This book is dedicated to the brave individuals, who over the course of four years, endured threats, surveillance, death threats, criminal prosecution, judicial persecution, passport confiscation, warrants, and imprisonment due to their investigation into the academic degree fraud scandal involving Taiwan's President Tsai Ing-wen and the London School of Economics and Political Science (LSE).

Title: Evils III
Editor-in-Chief: Dr. Dennis Peng
Publisher: Dennis Peng
First Edition Released: December 20, 2023
Price: USD $35
Published by: Thesis7ting LLC, USA
ISBN: 979-8-9897383-0-4
All rights reserved. Unauthorized reproduction will be pursued legally.

# Donate to
# "True Voice of Taiwan"

Donate via bank transfer ➜
Name: ECONOMIC AND POLITICAL MEDIA LIMITED
Address: 6F, No.125 Sec.3, Renai Rd., Taipei Taiwan
TEL: 886-2-27812266
Account number: 20032000051114
Bank name: Yuanta Commercial Bank Co., Ltd.
Bank address: 3F, No.210, Sec.3, Chengde Rd, Taipei, Taiwan
SWIFT Code：APBKTWTH

Donations from international viewers via PayPal ➜
https://www.paypal.me/truevot

United States: Mail checks to Weng Jeng Peng, 409 Tennant Station #215, Morgan Hill, CA 95037

您的支持是我們
一直前進的動力

More Information

# About Author

/Editor-in-Chief

## Dr. Dennis Peng

Bachelor from National Taiwan University, Master of Public Policy and Administration, and Doctorate in Journalism from the University of Wisconsin-Madison.

Dr. Peng's career spans roles as a reporter, news anchor, political talk show host, and producer. He was held academic positions as a Professor and the Director of the Graduate Institute of Journalism at National Taiwan University, as well as the Director of the Multimedia Research Center. His contributions extend to executive roles, including serving on the board of Taiwan Broadcasting System (TBS) and as the CEO of Hakka Television at the TBS. As an advocate for social justice, he was appointed as a member and spokesperson for the Prosecutor Evaluation Committee. In 2021, Dr. Peng received the "Star of Justice Award" from Canada for his investigative efforts in the "LSE Thesis-Gate Scandal" controversy.

Currently, Dr. Peng is notable for questioning the legitimacy of Tsai's degree and alleging collusion with the London School of Economics and Political Science. As a result of these allegations, he was subject to an arrest warrant in 2021, had his Taiwanese passport revoked, and now resides in the United States as a stateless person.

# Table of contents

| | |
|---|---|
| About Author | 3 |
| Chronicle of Events | 6 |
| UK Tribunal Court Reveals:<br>LSE Provided False Evidence to Taiwan's Court | 14 |
| A Message to Readers | 20 |
| The 'Disappeared' Thesis:<br>A Revelation by a Scholar from MIT | 24 |
| Office Emergency Meeting:<br>Internal Recommendations, Strategies, and Decisions at LSE | 43 |
| Seeking the Truth:The 2015 Investigators | 47 |
| The Genesis of the Storm:<br>A Photocopy of the 1985/86 Academic Regulations | 53 |
| The Strategy of Balancing Between LSE and<br>the Taiwan Presidential Office | 65 |
| Confidential Instructions:<br>Internal Struggle at the University of London | 73 |
| The Fog of Time:The Entanglement of 1984 and 2011 | 80 |
| LSE's Strategy of Ambiguity | 95 |
| The Obfuscation of Truth:<br>The Reality and Strategy Within LSE | 106 |
| The Conundrum of Three Certificates:<br>Renewed Doubts Over Tsai's Degree | 111 |

| | |
|---|---|
| The Enigma of the Black Leather-Bound Thesis:<br>Taiwan's Representatives Visit LSE | 122 |
| LSE's Strategy:<br>Canned Responses and Image Management | 127 |
| The Enigma of the Women's Library:<br>The Mystery of Tsai's Thesis Storage | 142 |
| LSE's Strategy in the Face of Scrutiny:<br>Blame it on Fake Accounts! | 172 |
| Certificates of "Evils I" in Major Libraries Worldwide | 195 |
| Appendix | 213 |
| List of Individuals Involved in LSE Thesis-gate Scandal | 227 |
| Epilogue | 244 |

## Chronicle of Events

**June 19, 2015**
A Taiwanese scholar from the Massachusetts Institute of Technology (MIT) wrote to the Canadian Sing Tao Daily with the headline "The Untraceable Doctoral Thesis of Tsai Ing-wen," stating that he couldn't locate President Tsai Ing-wen's thesis by any means.

**May 4, 2019**
Professor Hwan C. Lin, former President of the North American Taiwanese Professors' Association and Professor at the University of North Carolina at Charlotte's Business School, began an email inquiry into Tsai's missing thesis at the London School of Economics (LSE).

**May 20, 2019**
Professor He De-fen, an honorary professor at the National Taiwan University Law School, held a press conference raising questions about the unavailability of Tsai's thesis in libraries worldwide, sparking controversy in Taiwanese society.

**June 10, 2019**
Professor Dennis Peng, former director of the Institute of Journalism at National Taiwan University, commented on Facebook that this was the strangest incident he had encountered in his 25 years in academia.

**June 11, 2019**
Li Chung-Chih, President of the North American Taiwanese Professors' Association, sidestepped questions about the non-existence of the thesis and posted a photo of Tsai's LSE diploma, reissued in 2015, on Facebook.

**June 11, 2019**
Professor He made her first public disclosure about the doubts surrounding Tsai's thesis on the online show "True Voice of Taiwan," hosted by Professor Peng.

**June 28, 2019**
The electronic index of Tsai's thesis "Unfair Trade Practices and Safeguard Actions" appeared for the first time in the LSE electronic catalog, co-authored with Michael Elliott.

**July 10, 2019**
During an interview with the Taiwanese social media platform Dcard, Tsai flashed her "LSE Ph.D. diploma" for 20 seconds in front of the media.

**July 19, 2019**
The Ministry of Education sealed Tsai's faculty appointment and promotion records at Taiwan's Soochow University and National Chengchi University until December 31, 2049.

*Continued on the next page*

6  The biggest degree fraud case in human history

| | |
|---|---|
| August 27, 2019 | Professor Lin published a 50-page "Independent Investigation Report on Tsai Ing-wen's Thesis." |
| August 29, 2019 | The Presidential Office spokesperson Chang Tun-Han held a press conference announcing lawsuits against Professors Lin and He. |
| September 12, 2019 | Professor Peng voiced support for the two scholars on his daily talk show for a week. On the eve of the Mid-Autumn Festival, the Presidential Office issued a press release adding a lawsuit against Professor Peng. |
| September 18, 2019 | Dr. Hsu Yong-tai of Oxford University, after personally reviewing Tsai's so-called thesis, published his impressions in three parts in the World Journal He pointed out that the black book displayed in the LSE Women's Library was not an official thesis. Dr. Hsu also wrote to the LSE Law Department requesting an investigation into Tsai Ing-wen's doctoral records. The department responded that they did not retain any information on Tsai's doctoral studies. |
| September 19, 2019 | For the first time, Tsai Ing-wen responded to media inquiries about her degree controversy, emphasizing that if there's a degree, there's a thesis. |
| September 23, 2019 | The Presidential Office held its first press conference on the thesis controversy, presenting Tsai's thesis drafts page by page with white gloves. However, the paper's age did not match the content. On the same day, legislator Guan Bi-ling revealed Tsai's third diploma, reissued in 2010. Tsai Ing-wen had three diplomas, two of which were reissued, violating the University of London's one-time reissue rule. |
| September 24, 2019 | During her last media inquiry on the thesis controversy in Zuoying, Tsai reiterated that the thesis was not presented page by page but as a whole book. She also stated that the National Library had agreed to collect and publish the thesis.  |
| September 27, 2019 | The National Library, in violation of the Degree Conferral Law, included Tsai's so-called "Unfair trade practices and safeguard actions" thesis in the Master's Theses and Doctoral Dissertations section. |
| October 8, 2019 | The LSE official website posted a statement titled "LSE statement on Ph.D. of Dr Tsai Ing-wen." |

Continued on the next page

The biggest degree fraud case in human history

**October 14, 2019** — During a legislative inquiry, legislator Apollo Chen asked the 48 national university presidents present how many believed President Tsai's degree was genuine. In the end, only six university presidents raised their hands. Even Guo Mingzheng, the president of National Chengchi University where Tsai Ing-wen once taught, did not raise his hand.

**October 18, 2019** — Professor Peng led a group to London and conducted a firsthand investigation at the LSE library. They recorded interviews with library staff, proving that the library had never collected the thesis. On the same day, a press conference on the thesis scandal was held in London with Professor Lin.

**October 21, 2019** — U.S. independent journalist Michael Richardson filed a request under the Freedom of Information Act (FOIA) to LSE, seeking disclosure of Tsai's viva committee members and the date of her viva. LSE's Information Manager Rachel Maguire responded that the viva took place on October 16, 1983, which was a Sunday. She also mentioned that the related records are held by the University of London. Richardson then initiated a FOIA request with the University of London.

**October 31, 2019** — Professor Ou Ching-Chun discovered 79 errors in the six-page table of contents of what Tsai claims to be her "Ph.D. thesis."

**November 2, 2019** — On his show, former President Chen Shui-bian revealed that Tsai's 2015 graduation certificate was obtained through former Deputy Executive of the Council for Economic Planning and Development Huang Guo-jun, who personally traveled to the UK to "handle" the matter with former LSE Dean Anthony Giddens.

**November 4, 2019** — On the UK website WhatDoTheyKnow, a record of all donations to LSE from 2008 to 2014 was disclosed. Of the 600 entries, only one was an anonymous donation of 480,000 pounds, specifically designated for LSE Taiwan Research Programme researcher Shih Fang-long.

**November 9, 2019** — Netizens discovered a 2011 Facebook photo which included Tsai, the current Mayor of Kaohsiung Chen Qi-mai, Xiao Mei-qin, Xie Zhi-wei, Chen Qi-mai, and Zhang Xiao-yue. They were visiting LSE and met with former LSE Dean Anthony Giddens, Acting Dean Ms. Dame Judith Rees, and David Held, the advisor to Saif al-Islam Gaddafi, the Libyan leader involved in a Ph.D. scandal.

*Continued on the next page*

8    The biggest degree fraud case in human history

## 2019

**November 28, 2019**
Legislator Chen held a public hearing on the "Thesis Gate" at the Legislative Yuan. Researcher Yan Zhen-sheng from the National Chengchi University's Center for International Relations pointed out that Tsai's so-called thesis had 444 typos. The investigation into Tsai's degree was officially recorded in the official documents of the Taiwanese Parliament.

**December 5, 2019**
To avoid potential withdrawal of charges against him after the presidential election, Professor Peng filed two lawsuits against Tsai: one for defamation and the other to confirm the non-existence of the thesis. He also filed an aggravated defamation lawsuit against Presidential Office spokesperson Chang Tun-Han.

## 2020

**January 15, 2020**
Without holding a court session or providing any explanation, Judge Zhang Yong-hui of the Taipei District Court suddenly ruled on the lawsuit confirming the non-existence of the thesis, resulting in Professor Peng's loss.

**January 26, 2020**
In response to Richardson's FOIA request regarding Tsai's viva committee, the University of London refused to disclose the information, citing data protection laws. Richardson subsequently appealed to the UK Information Commissioner's Office (ICO).

**March 24, 2020**
Richardson received an investigative report from the ICO, stating that disclosing the viva committee would cause distress and damage to the parties involved. The report also mentioned that due to the pandemic, there might be delays in its release.

**June 11, 2020**
Richardson made public the case of Tsai's viva committee. The ICO arbitration result agreed with the University of London's decision not to disclose.
https://ico.org.uk/media/action-weve-taken/decision-notices/2020/2617860/fs50908339.pdf

This report, based on testimony from the University of London's Information Manager Kit Good, claimed that the University of London holds records of Tsai's thesis publication, viva report, and degree details. It also explained that Tsai's thesis was misplaced or lost during library renovations between the 1980s and 2010s. Kit Good unexpectedly resigned in September 2021. The ICO report further indicated that the thesis currently stored at LSE might be a draft. Richardson then appealed against the ICO to the UK Information Tribunal Court.

*Continued on the next page*

## 2020

**July 8, 2020** — Another ICO arbitration report was released, regarding the thesis that Tsai submitted only in 2019. The ICO concluded that this was a version of the thesis that had not undergone formal evaluation.

https://ico.org.uk/media/action-weve-taken/decision-notices/2020/2618008/fs50898869.pdf

**July 17, 2020** — The ICO, citing Richardson's non-British nationality, asked the Tribunal Court to reject his FOIA request. The case was temporarily frozen, pending resolution of the nationality dispute.

## 2021

**February 24, 2021** — The UK Administrative Court agreed that the FOIA does not pertain to nationality or territory. As long as one provides a real name and residence, the FOIA request to disclose Tsai's viva committee was unfrozen.

**March 27, 2021** — The ICO submitted four points of view to the court: (1) Tsai's personal privacy is more important than public information disclosure. (2) The court's power is limited, and the ICO is the final arbiter of data protection. (3) The 1985 Institute of Advanced Legal Studies (IALS) Law Index already provides sufficient information. (4) Taiwanese courts have already taken legal action against skeptics.

**March 31, 2021** — In Taiwan, Professor Peng was indicted by the Taipei District Prosecutor's Office for violating the Election and Recall Act and for aggravated defamation after being sued by President Tsai. Two other scholars, Professor He and Professor Lin, were not prosecuted.

**April 6, 2021** — In an unprecedented move, Professor Peng simultaneously received both an indictment and a non-prosecution notice from the Taipei District Prosecutor's Office.

**May 4, 2021** — The aggravated defamation case brought by Tsai against scholars had its first hearing at the Taipei District Court. Public prosecutor Huang Guan-yun indicted Peng mainly on the grounds of "why not believe Tsai." Outside the court, Peng and his lawyer Jim C. Chang criticized the hearing, saying, "All Taiwanese prosecutors have the surname Tsai."

*Continued on the next page*

**May 26, 2021** — Richardson made a second FOIA request to LSE, asking for the list of viva committee members. LSE's Board Secretary Louise Nadal, replied to Richardson, stating that the school does not hold the information requested. Richardson appealed to the ICO.

**September 13, 2021** — The FOIA request by Richardson to disclose Tsai's viva committee resulted in a First-tier Tribunal decision. After reviewing the undisclosed documents provided by the University of London, the court determined that they contained the names of Tsai's viva committee members. The court ruled in favor of the ICO, agreeing with the University of London's decision not to disclose. Richardson then appealed to the Upper Tribunal.

https://informationrights.decisions.tribunals.gov.uk/DBFiles/Decision/i2943/032%20200921%20Richardson%20EA%202020%200212%20p.pdf    First-tier Tribunal Judgment

**October 20, 2021** — In the lawsuit filed by Tsai against Professor Peng, the Taipei District Court entered the preparatory procedure. Professor Peng, the defendant who was visiting relatives in the US, applied for a video conference appearance due to the severe pandemic situation and threats to his personal safety. The court rejected his application without providing a reason. Prosecutor Liu Cheng-wu proposed a warrant for Professor Peng, asking him to appear in court to clarify any real malice. After Judge Yao Nian-ci raised questions about why the defendant did not appear in court and why there was no stamp from the defendant on the document, she immediately adjourned, leaving the audience in shock.

**November 19, 2021** — The Taipei District Court issued a 13-year warrant for Professor Peng without providing any legal justification.

**November 26, 2021** — Richardson made a second FOIA request to LSE, inquiring if LSE holds any records related to Tsai's Ph.D. viva. The ICO arbitrated that LSE denies having any such records and logically, the records should be held by the University of London.

https://ico.org.uk/action-weve-taken/decision-notices/ic-109451-s1m2/

*Continued on the next page*

The biggest degree fraud case in human history

## 2021

**December 18, 2021** — In response to the University of London's claim that Tsai's thesis was misplaced or lost during library renovations between 1980-2010, Tribunal Judge Hazel Oliver, after reviewing a library investigation video provided by Professor Peng, ruled that the claim of the thesis being lost was incorrect.

## 2022

**January 11, 2022** — Suzie Mereweather, the newly appointed Data Protection and Information Compliance Manager succeeding Kit Good at the University of London, responded on the WhatDoTheyKnow website, addressing why LSE's Record Manager Rachael Maguire, knew Tsai's viva date. Suzie Mereweather stated that the primary records of degree awards are held by member institutions, not the University of London.

https://www.whatdotheyknow.com/request/did_rachael_maguire_of_lse_get_t#incoming-1949200

On the same day, in response to an inquiry about the publication date of Tsai's thesis, Suzie Mereweather publicly admitted that the University of London never published Tsai's thesis, contradicting Kit Good's 2020 report to the ICO.

https://www.whatdotheyknow.com/request/the_publication_date_of_tsai_ing#incoming-1949227

**February 2, 2022** — The University of London released a statement on their official website regarding the missing thesis, stating that while it's unclear whether the thesis was stored in the university library, Tsai's doctoral degree was correctly awarded. However, the original statement mentioning the degree being awarded in February 1984 was later amended to March 1984.

**February 10, 2022** — Professors Peng, Lin, and He, jointly issued a statement, formally accusing the University of London and the LSE of covering up Tsai's Ph.D. degree fraud.

*Continued on the next page*

**June 21, 2022**

Regarding LSE's denial in the November 26, 2021 ICO arbitration report of holding any records related to Tsai's Ph.D. viva, Richardson appealed to the Tribunal Court and presented physical evidence from Professor Peng's indictment at the Taipei District Prosecutor's Office. In it, LSE's Legal Manager Kevin Haynes, testified to the Taipei District Court and provided the names of two viva examiners. LSE denied in court the evidence Haynes provided to the Taipei District Prosecutor's Office, stating it was obtained accidentally and its accuracy could not be confirmed. Tribunal Judge Alison Mckenna ruled that LSE must respond to Richardson's FOIA request within two weeks. LSE later changed its stance on Sempember 1, 2022, claiming exemption under data protection.

https://www.bailii.org/uk/cases/UKFTT/GRC/2022/2021_0373.html
First-tier Tribunal Judgment

**October 19, 2022**

The Taipei Economic and Cultural Office in San Francisco confiscated and revoked the valid passport of Professor Peng when he went to renew it, rendering him stateless and unable to board a plane.

**2023**

**March 3, 2023**

ICO Chief Commissioner John Edwards dismissed all FOIA requests questioning Tsai's degree as vexatious and deleted over a hundred questions and accounts on WhatDoTheyKnow.

**June 21, 2023**

Professor Lin made an FOIA request to LSE, asking which department of the school issued the university statement on October 8, 2019. The request was rejected by both LSE and ICO as vexatious. The first-instance Tribunal agreed with the ICO's view, considering it a frivolous action. Professor Lin appealed to the Upper Tribunal and won, sending the case back to the first-instance court, which was ordered to change the judge.

https://assets.publishing.service.gov.uk/media/64cd08bc9958270010c1e963/UA_2023_000363_GIA.pdf?fbclid=IwAR0cKVti2prHdpyoPTeXNyK4b6oQlo2IkrBnxnMY7Xvvpo0iLQZA8KZCM94

**August 22, 2023**

The UK investigative group Watchdog, based on the FOIA, released over 1000 internal emails from LSE covering up the scandal of Tsai's Ph.D. degree fraud on their website.

https://richardsonreport.com/

The biggest degree fraud case in human history    13

# UK Tribunal Court Reveals:
# LSE Provided False Evidence to Taiwan's Court

NCN

Case Reference: EA/2021/0373

**FIRST-TIER TRIBUNAL**
**GENERAL REGULATORY CHAMBER**
**INFORMATION RIGHTS**

Heard: By determination on the papers
Heard: On 13 June 2022
Decision Given on: 21 June 2022

|  |  |
|---|---|
| MICHAEL RICHARDSON | Appellant |
| - and - | |
| THE INFORMATION COMMISSIONER | Respondent |

Before:
JUDGE ALISON MCKENNA
SUSAN WOLF
DAN PALMER-DUNK

DECISION

1. The appeal is allowed.

2. Substituted Decision Notice:

A. **The Tribunal finds that Decision Notice IC-109451-SIM2 dated 26 November 2021 was erroneous and that information within the scope of the information request is held by LSE;**

B. **LSE must within 28 days issue a fresh response to the Appellant's original information request which confirms that information within the scope of his request is held and either disclose it or claim any exemptions to disclosure on which it relies.**

## REASONS

*Mode of Hearing*

3. The parties and the Tribunal agreed that this matter was suitable for determination on the papers in accordance with rule 32 of the Chamber's Procedure Rules[1].

4. The Tribunal considered an agreed open bundle of evidence comprising pages 1 to 86. It also considered submissions from the public authority, the Council of the London School of Economics and Science ('LSE') and further evidence and submissions from the Appellant.

*Background to Appeal*

5. The Appellant made a request to LSE on 2 May 2021 for the names of the examiners who examined the then Miss Tsai Ing-Wen (now President of Taiwan) for her PhD and the report from her viva.

6. LSE responded on 4 May and 26 May 2021 that it did not hold the requested information because at the relevant time (1984), it was the University of London which awarded degrees to LSE students.

7. The Information Commissioner issued Decision Notice IC-109451-SIM2 on 26 November 2021. It concluded on the balance of probabilities that the requested information was not held by LSE.

8. The Appellant appealed to the Tribunal. LSE was sent the appeal papers and invited to make submissions or to apply to be joined as a party to the appeal. It chose only to make submissions, but also supplied evidence.

*The Law*

9. S. 1(1)(a) of the Freedom of Information Act 2000 ('FOIA') provides that a person making an information request is entitled to be informed in writing whether the public authority holds information within the scope of the request. Where information within the scope of the request is held, it must either be disclosed or an exemption claimed.

---

[1] https://www.gov.uk/government/publications/general-regulatory-chamber-tribunal-procedure-rules

10. Where there is a dispute about whether information is held, the Tribunal makes a finding of fact on the evidence before it, applying the civil standard of proof, the balance of probabilities.

11. The Upper Tribunal's Decision in *Malnick v IC and ACOBA* [2018] UKUT 72 (AAC)[2], confirmed that a public authority must pass through the 'gateway' of compliance with ss. 1, 2 and 17 FOIA before being entitled to raise a late exemption before the Tribunal. As the public authority in this case stated that it did not hold the requested information, it has not yet claimed any applicable exemptions to disclosure. This means that the Tribunal cannot in this appeal decide whether any exemptions to disclosure apply.

12. The powers of the Tribunal in determining this appeal are set out in s.58 of FOIA, as follows:

> *"If on an appeal under section 57 the Tribunal considers -*
>
> *(a) that the notice against which the appeal is brought is not in accordance with the law, or*
> *(b) to the extent that the notice involved an exercise of discretion by the Commissioner, that he ought to have exercised his discretion differently,*
>
> *the Tribunal shall allow the appeal or substitute such other notice as could have been served by the Commissioner, and in any other case the Tribunal shall dismiss the appeal.*
>
> *On such an appeal, the Tribunal may review any finding of fact on which the notice in question was based."*

*Submissions and Evidence*

13. The Appellant's Notice of Appeal dated 14 December 2021 relied on grounds that (i) the Decision Notice was erroneous in concluding on the balance of probabilities that information was not held; (ii) that President Tsai's office has provided consent to the disclosure of any personal data on her student file; and (iii) that LSE has failed to comply with its legal obligations under FOIA. He requested that the Tribunal remits the matter to the Information Commissioner and directs a more thorough investigation.

14. The Information Commissioner's Response dated 19 January 2022 resisted the appeal and maintained the analysis set out in the Decision Notice. It is also submitted that, in another case on the subject of President Tsai's PhD (in which the public authority was the University of London), the Tribunal found that the names of the examiners were exempt from disclosure under s. 40 (2) FOIA. The Information Commissioner invited the Appellant to withdraw his appeal.

---

[2] 2018_AACR_29ws.pdf (publishing.service.gov.uk)

15. The Appellant's Reply made clear that he would not be withdrawing his appeal. He submits that the Information Commissioner had not informed him that it had any concerns about the provenance of a copy email he had provided dated 16 December 2020 and had simply failed to take it into account in reaching the conclusions in the Decision Notice. So that the Tribunal would not have similar concerns, he produced a further copy exhibited to an affidavit (see below). He addressed the question of the examiners' names being their personal data.

16. In response to the Registrar's Directions of 7 March 2022, LSE declined to be joined as a party to this appeal but made submissions and provided evidence. Its submission to the Tribunal dated 14 March 2022 it stated that "…*the information we hold on file is only there accidentally… we cannot be certain that this information is accurate*".

17. LSE confirmed to the Tribunal that it holds President Tsai's student file, comprising 278 pages. It stated that there is a letter on this file in which a person appears to self-identify as one of the Viva examiners, but that it has no official notification from University of London whether this information was correct, and it holds no information on the identity of the co-examiner. Commenting on the email of 16 December 2020 (see below), LSE states that its review found that the information provided by LSE in that email was *"likely inaccurate. This was based on a hurried view of a scanned file that cannot be key word searched. The email chain… is attached"*.

18. The Appellant made final submissions in which he asked the Tribunal to direct LSE to disclose pages from President Tsai's student file.

19. The Tribunal considered the following evidence, produced by the Appellant.

(i) An email dated 16 December 2020 in which a senior employee of LSE stated in an email that he had reviewed President Tsai's student file and *"…it appears from her student file that [XX][3] and [YY] examined President Tsai's thesis in October 1983"*.

(ii) The 16 December 2020 email was provided by the Appellant to the Information Commissioner's Office during its investigation, but it did not ask LSE about it, apparently being uncertain of its provenance. The Appellant provided the Tribunal with a further copy of the email, exhibited to an affidavit dated 24 January 2022 signed by journalist Dennis Peng, who states he obtained it via disclosure during defamation proceedings brought against him by President Tsai and that the addressee of the email is *"the inquiry of the Taiwanese Judiciary Institution"* which is investigating President Tsai's PhD.

---

[3] We have here anonymized the persons named as a precaution in view of the Tribunal's Decision referred to in paragraph 14, although we note we are not bound to take the same view. We understand that the Appellant has seen these names in full because they were provided to the Tribunal unredacted.

(iii) The Appellant also relied on evidence in the form of an email dated 12 June 2019, in which President Tsai's office gave LSE consent to the disclosure of personal data in her student file.

(iv) The Appellant produced an email dated 14 June 2019 from a member of staff at LSE to President Tsai's office in which there is a reference to "fending off" enquiries about President Tsai's PhD. The Appellant relies on this as evidence that LSE is reluctant to comply with its duties under FOIA.

20. The Tribunal considered the following evidence, provided by LSE with its submissions of 14 March 2022:

An internal email dated 31 March 2021, addressed to the member of staff who sent the 16 December 2020 email, as follows:

*Looking at it again, I was wondering where in the student file you got the information that she had two internal examiners – [XX] and [YY] – and one external examiner – [ZZ].*

*As far as I can see the only examiners referred to in the file are:*

*-[ZZ], named as external examiner in a letter from Pres Tsai to ...Sec of Graduate School at LSE, 5 December 1983*

*-[XX], who refers to 'my co-examiner and myself' in a memo ... dated 16/1/1983. This also suggests there were only two examiners, [XX] and one other.*

*I see [YY] is mentioned in the file but couldn't find him specifically named as an examiner.*

21. We have not seen the reply to that email. We note that LSE has not disputed that the email of 16 December 2020 was sent, only that it now doubts the accuracy of its contents.

*Conclusion*

22. The Decision Notice concluded on the balance of probabilities that LSE did not hold the requested information. The Tribunal has had the benefit of additional evidence provided by the Appellant and by LSE itself with its submissions.

23. We conclude on the basis of all the evidence before us and on the balance of probabilities that information within the scope of the request is held by LSE in President Tsai's student file. That information has been referred to in email correspondence between LSE and others (including apparently being supplied to a judicial inquiry) and is also referred to in its submission to the Tribunal. We understand that LSE doubts the accuracy of this information, but we conclude that this is not a basis for stating that information is not held under FOIA.

24. It may be that exemptions will be claimed, but we conclude that LSE must now issue a fresh response in which that issue is addressed. As we have concluded that information is held, the correct course is for LSE to issue a fresh response on the basis that information within the scope of the request is held, and at that stage either disclose the requested information (with contextual commentary, if necessary) or claim any exemptions to disclosure that it considers apply. If the Appellant disagrees with that response, he may complain to the Information Commissioner. The Tribunal may only become involved if a further Decision Notice is issued.

25. We allow this appeal on the basis of the Appellant's first ground of appeal, that the Decision Notice was erroneous in its conclusion that information was not held.

26. As to the Appellant's second ground of appeal, we note that President Tsai may only give permission to disclose her own personal data and may not override the privacy rights of third parties. In any event, this Tribunal may not determine the applicability of exemptions which have not yet been claimed and have not been considered in a Decision Notice.

27. As to the Appellant's third ground, this Tribunal's jurisdiction extends only to considering the Decision Notice. It is not our role to comment on LSE's handling of the request.

28. We now allow the appeal and make the substituted Decision Notice above.


(Signed)

**JUDGE ALISON MCKENNA**　　　　　　　　**DATE: 20 June 2022**


© CROWN COPYRIGHT 2022

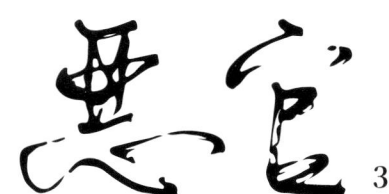

## A Message to Readers

# A Message to Readers

After four and a half years of investigation into the odd occurrences between the London School of Economics and the Office of the President in Taiwan, do our findings align with academic standards and logic?

1. Does LSE allow a Ph.D. dissertation advisor to have only a bachelor's degree in an unrelated field?

2. Is it feasible for both Ph.D. oral examination committee members to be internal faculty of the University of London, with no external examiners?

3. Does having a supervisor serve as an examiner violate University of London regulations?

4. Is it conceivable that an LSE Ph.D. dissertation has never been cited, not even by the author?

5. As LSE claims, could the oral examination date be on October 16, 1983, which was a Sunday?

6. Isn't the notation of WD (financial difficulties) on November 10, 1982, in the student record an abbreviation for withdrawal?

7. Can a student who withdrew acquire a Ph.D. the following year?

8. If LSE records show no tuition payments for 1983, is it likely that the oral examination and subsequent awarding of a degree happened in 1984?

9. Can the vast majority of the 287-page student record submitted by the Office of the President in Taiwan in 2019 serve as proof of a doctoral degree?

10. Is an oral examination conceivable without the prior submission of the required entry form?

11. Can a student submit a thesis for examination within five months of their topic approval in January 1983?

12. Has there ever been a case in LSE where a thesis required no revisions after the oral examination?

13. Can an LSE dissertation have 79 errors in the table of contents and 444 typos throughout?

14. Is it plausible for the Acknowledgement section of an LSE Ph.D. thesis to misspell the advisor's name?

15. Would LSE allow a doctoral thesis to have over two hundred pencil and correction fluid amendments?

16. Is an LSE doctoral thesis permissible to be typed in different fonts?

17. Could the footnotes of an LSE doctoral thesis from 1984 contain references to articles published after that year?

18. Can an LSE thesis be partly left-justified, right-justified, and fully justified?

19. Can LSE translate a thesis verbatim over 200 pages from two Chinese journals (National Taiwan University Law Journal and Soochow Law Journal)?

20. Why has LSE yet to initiate any investigation despite confirming via email that the 2015 diploma that was reissued was fake?

21. As Tsai claims in her autobiography, is it true that LSE awarded her 1.5 doctoral degrees?

22. Does LSE allow a graduate of 35 years to submit their own claimed academic records to the student file?

23. Can LSE accept forged documents submitted by an alumna 35 years post-graduation for inclusion in their file as a basis for credential verification?

24. Can LSE provide incorrect information to Taiwanese judicial authorities for false testimony without legal repercussions?

25. Can LSE and the University of London endorse a doctoral degree without records of the oral examination committee members, especially

22  The biggest degree fraud case in human history

when no library in the world has a microfilm copy of Tsai's 1984 dissertation?

26. Can someone teaching at Soochow University in Taiwan in September 1983 have attended an oral examination at LSE on October 16 of the same year?

27. In her autobiography, Tsai mentions that her thesis was so well written that her supervisor and examiners debated whether to award her one or two doctoral degrees, ultimately deciding on 1.5 degrees (https://youtu.be/_oJnyMk1h_8). Is there any precedent for this at LSE?

28. Can someone be employed as an LSE lecturer without a record of their Ph.D. in the LSE personnel files?

29. Why did LSE state they could not find the 1984 thesis in their library due to a clerical error, only to later claim it was misplaced during the 1980s renovations?

30. How could Tsai's thesis, purportedly lost during the 1980s renovations, be located intact in 2015 with annotations in pencil?

This book is an appeal for academic integrity and a call for justice in the face of corruption and abuse of power. It seeks to uncover the truth and hold those accountable who have compromised educational standards for political gain.

# The 'Disappeared' Thesis:
# A Revelation by a Scholar from MIT

# The 'Disappeared' Thesis:
# A Revelation by a Scholar from MIT

In 2019, a controversy over the educational credentials of Taiwanese President Tsai Ing-wen caused ripples across the international academic community. Tsai's qualifications became a focal point during the election, drawing in several influential figures from academia.

On June 19, 2015, a Taiwanese scholar at the Massachusetts Institute of Technology published an opinion piece in Canada's Sing Tao Daily titled "The Untraceable Doctoral Thesis of Tsai Ing-wen," asserting that despite exhaustive efforts, Tsai's doctoral thesis could not be located. This article did not initially shake the academic world.

However, on May 4, 2019, the investigation into the missing thesis was revived by Hwan C. Lin, a professor at the University of North Carolina at Charlotte's Belk College of Business and former president of the North American Taiwanese Professors' Association. Soon after, He De-fen, an emeritus law professor at National Taiwan University, joined the inquiry and held a press conference on May 20, claiming that Tsai's thesis was nowhere to be found in global libraries, sparking widespread attention and skepticism.

Subsequently, Changqing Cao, an American political commentator, questioned the authenticity of Tsai's credentials on the show "Cross-Strait Politics and Economics." In response, Professor Dennis Peng, the former director of National Taiwan University's Graduate Institute of Journalism, stated on Facebook that this was the most bizarre incident he had encountered in his 25 years in academia.

On June 11, 2019, the then-president of the North America Taiwanese Professors' Association, Li Chung-Chih, posted photos of Tsai's 2015 reissued LSE diploma on Facebook in Tsai's defense. However, the same day, Professor He revealed doubts about the thesis scandal on the show "Cross-Strait Politics and Economics."

Clive Wilson, the Enquiry Services Manager at the London School of Economics and Political Science (LSE), was at the heart of the storm. Wilson, who had been involved in LSE's internal investigation of Tsai's thesis in 2015, realized from the outset that the controversy was not just about a thesis but involved issues of academic integrity, political elections, and national image. He decided to lead the team in adopting an approach befitting international relations by providing a unified statement to quell the controversy. Initially, LSE decided to dismiss inquiries with a simple response, only stating known facts that the library never had Tsai's thesis and offered no explanation regarding the degree.

The issue took an unexpected turn when the Taiwan Presidential Office submitted an electronic version and a hard copy of Tsai's thesis, hoping to validate her educational background. Fang-long Shih, co-director of the Taiwan Research Programme at LSE, representing the Taiwan Presidential Office, contacted LSE for a list of examiners and advisors, aiming for a deeper understanding to rationalize the dispute.

The communications between Wilson and Shih became the focal point of the uproar. Wilson indicated that if the Taiwan Presidential Office could provide an electronic copy of the thesis, they could assist in its incorporation into the library to affirm its authenticity. However, an anonymous letter later arrived in the hands of Shih and Wilson, requesting the thesis not be made public and hoping LSE would state support of President Tsai.

Faced with such pressure, Wilson obtained the thesis title and acknowledgments page from the Taiwan Presidential Office, hoping to find clues about the thesis advisor and the examiners. The storm continued to escalate, with accusatory letters being sent to the LSE Executive office. Amidst this, Wilson suggested using the material the Taiwan Presidential Office provided to clarify the controversy. However, due to many doubts, LSE's Media Relations Manager Daniel O'connor joined the fray, aiming for a unified response to avoid further complications. At the same time, Wilson proposed an internal discussion on minimizing other inquiries rather than revealing the truth.

On June 28, 2019, Tsai's thesis *Unfair Trade Practices and Safeguard Actions*, co-authored with Michael Elliott, appeared for the first time in LSE's electronic catalog, reigniting widespread attention and discussion.

Against this backdrop, Marcus W. Cerny, the Deputy Head of Doctoral Programmes at LSE, believed that, apart from the public interest, there was a need for more cautious information dissemination. Wilson decided to convene a confidential internal meeting to discuss handling the matter, ultimately leading to one of the most significant and far-reaching academic fraud scandals in history.

# FW_ FYI - LSE Ph.D. thesis Taiwan president

**From:** Wilson,Clive
**Sent:** 11 June 2019 12:35
**To:** Bell,M; Bhullar,J; Challis,D; Collings,R; Dawson,H; Fry,AE; Gomes,S; Graham1,N; Hayward,S; Horsler,PN; Hussain,R; Murphy,GE; Orson,R; Payne1,D; Reid,MJ; Towlson,A; Wilkinson,E; Wilson,Clive; Zajasensky,L; Benton,A; Rodriguez; Poulose,S; Donnelly,S; Wilson1,K; Griffiths,CB
**Cc:** Lsethesesonline
**Subject:** LSE PhD thesis - Taiwan president

Hi All

sorry to send this so widely, but I'm trying to cover all bases. Please forward if you think I've missed anyone.

There are presidential primaries in Taiwan this week to decide who the candidate for the DPP will be. One is the current president and LSE alumna Ing-wen Tsai.

Ing-wen Tsai received her PhD from LSE in 1984: Unfair trade practices and safeguard actions.

We have had three queries in the last two weeks about it.

There was also great interest in it when she first stood for election and we had to do a lot of digging. LSE Library has never had a copy and Senate House could not find their copy. We tried IALS as some law theses went there but they didn't have it either. The student record was checked and LSE is satisfied that the PhD was awarded correctly.

The standard response to any query about the thesis is as follows:

> Thank you for expressing an interest in this thesis. Unfortunately, LSE Library has never had a copy of this thesis. All PhDs from that period were awarded under the University of London banner and would have been sent first to Senate House Library. As you can appreciate there has been a lot of interest in Dr Tsai's thesis, we have been in correspondence with the University of London about it and extensive checks have been made. Unfortunately Senate House are unable to find their copy.
>
> I am sorry we cannot help further.

But please copy any queries to both me and lsethesesonline@lse.ac.uk

thanks

Clive

**From:** Wright,NC
**Sent:** 11 June 2019 15:54
**To:** Pressoffice <Pressoffice@lse.ac.uk>
**Cc:** Nadal,L <L.Nadal@lse.ac.uk>; Hix,S <S.Hix@lse.ac.uk>; Thomson,MT <M.T.Thomson@lse.ac.uk>
**Subject:** FYI - LSE PhD thesis - Taiwan president

Dear all,

Just a quick alert that the Library has been receiving queries about this alum and the PhD. This happened a few years ago and Simeon Underwood at that time investigated and established these details. We are responding as per the below text. This could be high profile during the election period in Taiwan.

Best wishes,
Nicola

# FW_-Greetings-from-the-Presidential-office-of-Tsai

**From:** ▇▇▇▇▇▇▇▇▇▇
**Date:** Wednesday, 12 June 2019 at 09:08
**To:** "Wilson,Clive" <CLIVE.Wilson@lse.ac.uk>
**Cc:** "Shih,I " <I.Shih@lse.ac.uk>
**Subject:** Greetings from the Presidential office of Taiwan

Dear Mr. Clive Wilson,

I extend my cordial greetings to you.

As you might already be aware of the recent argument with respect to the admission of Taiwan President Tsai, Ing-Wen's PhD degree awarded by LSE in 1983. We note that LSE

has taken actions to identify related documentation in this regard. On behalf of President Tsai, I would like to give consent to the disclosure of personal information in her PhD thesis, "Unfair Trade Practice and Safeguard Actions."

Further, we are able to provide both the electronic and hardbound editions of the subject thesis for the library collection upon your request. Please kindly let us know if this is feasible at your convenience.

Thank you for your assistance on this matter.

Sincerely yours,
▇▇▇▇▇▇▇
Spokesperson of the President
Office of the President, ROC(Taiwan)
No.122, Sec.1,Chingqing S.Rd, Taipei City, Taiwan

**From:** Shih,F
**Sent:** 12 June 2019 09:47
**To:** Wilson,Clive
**Cc:** ███
**Subject:** Re: Greetings from the Presidential office of Taiwan

Dear Clive,

As suggested, President Tsai Ing-wen has now given her consent for the school to the disclosure of personal information related to her PhD thesis, entitled "Unfair Trade Practice and Safeguard Actions." Please see below the permission message.

As such, please add these information in the school letter: (1)

the names of her supervisor and viva examiners; (2) upon request, the electronic and hardbound editions of her PhD thesis will arrive at the LSE library.

As such, please give the address and the name where and who to receive this thesis. Many thanks!

Dear ███,

When will the electronic and hardbound editions of her PhD thesis be posted?

How long will it take from Taiwan to the LSE?

Many thanks!
Fang-long


Dr Fang-long Shih
Co-Director, Taiwan Research Programme
London School of Economics and Political Science
Houghton Street
London WC2A 2AE
United Kingdom

LSE Taiwan Research Programme
http://www.lse.ac.uk/researchAndExpertise/units/TaiwanProgramme/Home.aspx

Journal *Taiwan in Comparative Perspective*
http://www.lse.ac.uk/researchAndExpertise/units/TaiwanProgramme/Journal/Home.aspx

**From:** Wilson,Clive
**Sent:** 12 June 2019 09:56
**To:** Shih,F
**Cc:** 
**Subject:** RE: Greetings from the Presidential office of Taiwan

Dear Both

If there is an electronic copy, we can almost certainly catalogue it from that and make it available if it is a decent copy.

A hardbound copy can be sent to me at

Clive Wilson
Enquiry Services Manager (Academic Services)
London School of Economics
10 Portugal Street
London WC2A 2HD

It might not be a quick thing to retrieve President Tsai's student record and make the information available but I have asked if that is possible

Fang-long – are you still coming here at 10?

Clive

**From:** ▓▓▓▓▓▓▓▓▓▓▓▓▓▓▓▓▓▓
**Sent:** 12 June 2019 11:34
**To:** Shih,F
**Cc:** Wilson,Clive
**Subject:** RE: Greetings from the Presidential office of Taiwan

Dear Both,

Thank you so much for your kind assistance and understanding.

We are sending the hardbound editions of the subject thesis tomorrow and I believe it will arrive by next week. As for the electronic copy, we will email it to you by Friday. Please only use it for the LSE internal check not for the public release at this stage as it is indeed likely going to invite more irrational speculations.

LSE is one of the leading academic institutions in the world, and any statement issued by LSE certainly carries weight by itself. We truly appreciate your assistance and help us defend President Tsai's academic credential.

Sincerely,
▓▓▓▓

**Sent:** Wednesday, June 12, 2019 6:12 PM
**To:** Wilson,Clive <CLIVE.Wilson@lse.ac.uk>
**Cc:**
**Subject:** Re: Greetings from the Presidential office of Taiwan

Dear Clive,

Thank you. It is possible to get the electronic copy of the thesis today.

However, unfortunately, to make the electronic copy available at http://etheses.lse.ac.uk/ with other LSE theses will not end the speculation but invite many more 'irrational' speculations from anti-Tsai's camp.

As such, is it OK only to mention the arrival of the hardbound copy of the thesis.

However, the Presidential Office is ok to send you the electronic copy now, but please only use it for the LSE internal check not for the public release. I hope you could understand the fragile situation under the irrational attack now.

Many thanks,
Fang-long

**From:** Wilson,Clive
**Sent:** 17 June 2019 11:18
**To:** Cerny,MW; O'Connor,D; Graham1,N; Kelloway,C
**Subject:** FW: Greetings from the Presidential office of Taiwan

Dear All

we have been sent the title and acknowledgement page (attached) of the thesis from President Tsai's office with the promise we will receive a complete copy later this week..

Not sure how much these help at the moment although it clearly confirms who her supervisor was. Michael J Elliott passed away in 2016.

https://www.weforum.org/people/michael-j-elliott
https://en.wikipedia.org/wiki/Michael_J._Elliott

Also thanked:

Brian Hindley (LSE) passed away in 2012:
http://www.lse.ac.uk/newsletters/pressAndInformation/staffNews/2012/20120614.htm

▮▮▮▮▮▮▮▮▮▮▮▮▮▮▮▮▮▮▮▮▮▮▮▮▮▮▮▮▮▮▮▮▮▮▮▮▮▮

However, the Michael Elliott links show he left LSE for the Economist in 1984. This fits with what ▮▮▮▮ from UL sent us (copied again below) that Mr Elliott left both copies with LSE asking LSE to return them to Senate House. It's only circumstantial evidence but one could easily see them being left in his office and that being cleared out ...

I also wonder whether it's worth contacting ▮▮▮▮▮▮▮▮ to let him know of the interest. Even if we only ever make the print copy available through the archives reading room, his name is still likely to 'get out there'

Clive

Clive Wilson
Enquiry Services Manager (Academic Services)
London School of Economics      Tel.:   020 7955 7475
10 Portugal Street              Fax.:   020 7955 7454
London WC2A 2HD                 Email:  Datalibrary@lse.ac.uk
                                        clive.wilson@lse.ac.uk

**From:** Wilson,Clive
**Sent:** 17 June 2019 16:16
**To:** Cerny,MW; O'Connor,D; Graham1,N; Kelloway,C
**Subject:** RE: Greetings from the Presidential office of Taiwan
**Sensitivity:** Confidential

Hi everyone

sorry – me again!

After discussion with Rachel Maguire, Sue Donnelly sent me a copy of Tsai Ing-Wen's student file but with the caveat I can't even share it internally without Dr Tsai's further permission.

I have copied two pages from it though and, as I have permission from her office, I think these could be released if it was thought they would be helpful.

Clive

**From:** Cerny,MW
**Sent:** 17 June 2019 16:51
**To:** Kelloway,C; Wilson,Clive; O'Connor,D; Graham1,N
**Cc:** Metcalfe,F
**Subject:** RE: Greetings from the Presidential office of Taiwan
**Sensitivity:** Confidential

Dear Charlotte,

We have just received another query seeking the thesis in the PhD Academy but I am intending to simply reply with the standard response. I am assuming that we are not needing to refer these on for response from a single point but please could you confirm.

I have asked for all queries either here or in the Law department to be forwarded to me but I expect that the Library is the standard point of contact for external enquirers requesting a thesis.

Regards,
Marcus

**Marcus Cerny**
*Deputy Director, PhD Academy*
*London School of Economics and Political Science*
*Houghton Street*
*London WC2A 2AE*

<u>Please consider the environment and do not print this email unless absolutely necessary.</u>
Please access the attached hyperlink for an important electronic communications disclaimer:
http://lse.ac.uk/emailDisclaimer

**From:** Wilson,Clive
**Sent:** 21 June 2019 10:38
**To:** Cerny,MW; Kelloway,C; O'Connor,D; Graham1,N; Thomson,MT
**Cc:** Metcalfe,F
**Subject:** RE: Greetings from the Presidential office of Taiwan
**Sensitivity:** Confidential

Thanks Marcus

I feel this is one of those times it would be easier for us all to get together!

I understand the need for caution but she did win her party nomination and the elections are in January so this could run for a bit yet. ███████████████████████████████
████████████████████████████████████████████████████████████████
████████

████████████████████████████████████████████████████████████████
████████████████████████████████ I was introduced to her office by Fang-long and already have permission from her office to release her information as appropriate. If an amended release would be helpful – both to us and to her – we could therefore seek specific permission on that statement. (And I asked Info Sec to confirm that it was her office.)

I would completely agree that I'm not the person to decide what we might release or to whom. I hope it was clear mine was just a suggestion 😊 . I am hoping that if we do receive the promised copy that will kill most of the speculation but then Mike Elliott's name as well as Brian Hindley and ████████ ████████████ will get out there anyway.

Clive

**From:** Cerny,MW
**Sent:** 20 June 2019 16:50
**To:** Wilson,Clive; Kelloway,C; O'Connor,D; Graham1,N; Thomson,MT
**Cc:** Metcalfe,F
**Subject:** RE: Greetings from the Presidential office of Taiwan
**Sensitivity:** Confidential

Dear Clive,

Thanks for this.

I am a bit concerned about providing details about a registration, examination and processes to third parties. I would not release information for any candidates without their approval and even then it would be limited to registration dates and award details.

I understand that this case needs additional consideration because of the public interest aspect but I still feel the need for caution about what we should and shouldn't release. Other than what is in the public domain I would not discuss information with a third party about any current student or a graduate. I believe that these would be matters for them to respond to and would be of the opinion that a review of the file was undertaken by Simeon as the Academic Registrar in 2015 which concluded that he was satisfied that there was not an issue of the registration or award being in any way questionable. I am not sure it is appropriate to enter into discussion about this other than to confirm the award and that LSE is satisfied with this.

I've copied to Mark Thomson as his predecessor was the last person to review the file formally. It may be that either he or I should review this to make sure that any dates we are discussing are definitively correct. What we might release and to whom is a separate discussion but I would be more comfortable discussing this knowing we definitely had the correct timeline.

My main question now is who decides what we release and to whom?

Thanks,
Marcus


*Marcus Cerny*
*Deputy Director, PhD Academy*
*London School of Economics and Political Science*
*Houghton Street*
*London WC2A 2AE*

Please consider the environment and do not print this email unless absolutely necessary.
Please access the attached hyperlink for an important electronic communications disclaimer:
http://lse.ac.uk/emailDisclaimer

**From:** Wilson,Clive
**Sent:** 24 June 2019 09:38
**To:** Adeyemi,R
**Subject:** RE: Greetings from the Presidential office of Taiwan
**Sensitivity:** Confidential

Hi Remi

as follows – I've also attached a summary of Ing-Wen Tsai's students record.

Clive

On the 4<sup>th</sup> June (2019) a junior colleague sent our standard text to a US professor. He shared the text with some of his colleagues and suddenly it makes the Taiwanese news – with our member of staff's name attached. After several representations (about a week), her name was removed.

We have since had at least 22 requests that I am aware of: most of have come directly to the Library as it's a thesis (but to several departments here), but they have also gone to registry, the PhD Academy, Minouche ...

We have been replying with:

> Thank you for your email. We have checked our records and both the London School of Economics and Political Science and the University of London confirm that Tsai Ing-Wen was awarded a PhD in Law 1984.

> However, all PhDs from that period were awarded under the University of London banner and would have been sent first to their Senate House Library. We have been in correspondence with the University of London about the thesis and extensive checks have been made. Unfortunately, Senate House are presently unable to find their copy.

Most of the people have come back with further questions.

The issue of course is that we were never able to find a copy of her thesis. When she first stood for office in 2015, it blew over fairly quickly. Now she has stood for (and won) her party's nomination to run again with the elections in January it seems to have become much more of a story.

███████████ at UL confirmed in 2015 that 3 copies were submitted. Senate House and IALS lost one copy between them, but not before it was catalogued and so it is listed in all the places you would expect to see a thesis listed. The external examiner left his copy with the supervisor (Michael Elliott). Michael Elliott appears to have been away from LSE in the last year of her PhD (sabbatical?) and subsequently left LSE in 1984 to join the Economist having left instructions to pass them on. Clearly this never happened.

███████████████████████████████████████████████
███████████████████████████████████████████████
███████████████████████████████████████████████
███████████████████████

Fang-long Shih in the Taiwan Research Programme put me in touch with President Tsai's office and she sent copies of her title page and the acknowledgments page. We have been promised a full copy.

Our current reply confirms that the degree was awarded in 1984 but the non-existence of the thesis invites further questions. Her supervisor being the main one – Michael Elliott passed away in 2016.

The question – to me – is whether we continue to straight bat further queries which will hopefully go away if we receive a copy and make it available like all other print theses, or whether we release additional information to answer some of the questions people are asking.

**From:** ▮▮▮▮▮▮▮▮▮▮▮▮▮▮▮▮▮▮▮▮▮
**Sent:** 29 June 2015 15:13
**To:** ▮▮▮▮▮▮
**Cc:** Wilson,Clive; Lsethesesonline
**Subject:** RE: PhD LSE Law Thesis 1984
**Importance:** High

Dear ▮▮▮▮

My colleague has now retrieved the file on this student from our Archive Storage. From this I can see the history of chasing for copies of the thesis both by the Research Degrees Examinations office at Senate House and enquiries from Senate House Library too. In 2011 the SHL confirmed that it sent a copy of the thesis to the Institute for Advanced Legal Studies. At that time, ▮▮▮▮▮▮▮▮▮▮▮▮▮▮▮▮▮▮▮▮▮▮▮▮▮▮▮▮▮▮▮▮ established that IALS no longer had a copy of the said thesis.

The Research Degrees Examinations office had also chased both examiners (appointed for the PD examination) and the supervisor (Mr M J Elliott) for the return of the copies of the thesis. Apparently, the Internal Examiner left his copy of the PhD thesis with Mr Elliott post-viva. Mr Elliott left both copies with the LSE asking the LSE to return these to Senate House. These were never received.

The copy referred to above which went over to IALS would have been the spare third copy submitted to the Research Degrees Examinations office for examination on 15 June 1983.

I am sorry I cannot be more helpful.

With best wishes,

Lorraine

惡官 3

## Office Emergency Meeting: Internal Recommendations, Strategies, and Decisions at LSE

# Office Emergency Meeting: Internal Recommendations, Strategies, and Decisions at LSE

Wilson hastily drafted a unified response for external inquiries. Shortly after, Cerny received Wilson's draft. He believed the response must underscore that Tsai had indeed earned her degree, which was verified by both the University of London and LSE. This critical piece of information could defend the institution and quell external skepticism.

After several discussions and revisions, LSE finalized a unified external response, adding crucial information affirming Tsai's degree attainment. This information undeniably served as a potent rebuttal to public scrutiny.

However, the controversy was far from over. Wilson decided to instruct O'Connor to use the index of the British Library to lead the public into believing that Tsai's thesis had always existed. He hoped this would buy the institution more time and ward off further questioning.

Yet, a pointed question was raised: How could a degree be conferred if the thesis was not accepted? This query plunged LSE into a quandary. After internal discussions, LSE decided not to respond to this question.

In the meantime, Sue Donnelly, the Archivist from the LSE Secretary's Division, discovered a document from pages 43-46 of Tsai's student record, dated 1987 and signed by P.C. Kennedy from the Central Registry Office. She suggested that LSE and the University of London could disclose this document to defend the institution.

Nevertheless, the provenance of Tsai's so-called 278-page student record remained unclear. In a Tribunal Court judgment by Judge Alison McKenna on June 21, 2022, LSE admitted to the inaccuracy of the data, which was acquired serendipitously.

# FW_-Greetings-from-the-Presidential-office-of-Tsai

**From:** O"Connor,D
**To:** Metcalfe,F
**Subject:** FW: Ing-Wen Tsai's PhD thesis
**Date:** 11 June 2019 14:06:00

FYI

**From:** Cerny,MW
**Sent:** 11 June 2019 14:03
**To:** Graham1,N <N.Graham1@lse.ac.uk>; Orson,R <R.Orson@lse.ac.uk>
**Cc:** O'Connor,D <D.O'Connor@lse.ac.uk>; Wilson,Clive <CLIVE.Wilson@lse.ac.uk>; Lsethesesonline <Lsethesesonline@lse.ac.uk>
**Subject:** RE: Ing-Wen Tsai's PhD thesis

Hi Nancy,

The examination went through the University of London procedures and we had the award confirmed from them with a March 1984 award date. It was recorded in the 1985/86 Calendar and is recorded in both on LSE and U of L records.

Thanks,
Marcus

Marcus Cerny
*Deputy Director, PhD Academy*
*London School of Economics and Political Science*
*Houghton Street*
*London WC2A 2AE*

Please consider the environment and do not print this email unless absolutely necessary.
Please access the attached hyperlink for an important electronic communications disclaimer:
http://lse.ac.uk/emailDisclaimer

**From:** Graham1,N
**Sent:** 11 June 2019 13:58
**To:** Cerny,MW; Orson,R
**Cc:** O'Connor,D; Wilson,Clive; Lsethesesonline
**Subject:** RE: Ing-Wen Tsai's PhD thesis

Hi all

My colleague Clive Wilson has sent out some advice on this very issue today. He's drafted the following text for anyone to use if they receive a query. Clive has asked that if you do receive a query and reply, to copy both him and LSE Theses Online in – lsethesesonline@lse.ac.uk

> Thank you for expressing an interest in this thesis. Unfortunately, LSE Library has never had a copy of this thesis. All PhDs from that period were awarded under the University of London banner and would have been sent first to Senate House Library. As you can appreciate there has been a lot of interest in Dr Tsai's thesis, we have been in correspondence with the University of London about it and extensive checks have been made. Unfortunately Senate House are unable to find their copy.

**From:** Griffiths,CB
**Sent:** 13 June 2019 14:07
**To:** Kelloway,C
**Cc:** Orson,R; Metcalfe,F; Clark1,B; Wilson,Clive; O'Connor,D
**Subject:** RE: Ing-Wen Tsai's PhD thesis
**Importance:** High

Dear Charlotte,

I believe the press statement has been released which is good news – however Ruth's name is still appearing on the People's News web page. (https://www.peoplenews.tw/news/41075ad6-3253-4db4-a689-38d8ea3e1e1f)

Can you please let Ruth (and I) know where we are in relation to getting it removed? And can this be followed up if they do have not taken it down today?

Thanks,
Camilla

**From:** Kelloway,C
**Sent:** 12 June 2019 14:05
**To:** Wilson,Clive
**Cc:** Griffiths,CB; O'Connor,D; Metcalfe,F
**Subject:** RE: Ing-Wen Tsai's PhD thesis

Hi Clive,

We've adapted the reply to members of the public who are getting in touch. Please see below. Happy for you to send this out this out in reply to any general enquires, although do let us know if you would prefer this to come from us.

**General response:**

Thank you for your email. We have checked our records and both the London School of Economics and Political Science and the University of London confirm that Tsai Ing-Wen was awarded a PhD in Law 1984.

However, all PhDs from that period were awarded under the University of London banner and would have been sent first to their Senate House Library. We have been in correspondence with the University of London about the thesis and extensive checks have been made. Unfortunately, Senate House are presently unable to find their copy.

Kinds regards,

惡官 3

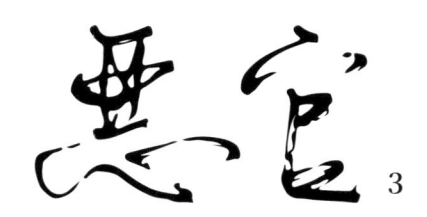

# Seeking the Truth:
# The 2015 Investigators

# Seeking the Truth: The 2015 Investigators

O'Connor was in the process of ascertaining the college's unified public statement. At the heart of this controversy lay the identity of Tsai's dissertation supervisor. Wilson knew that data protection laws do not cover information about the deceased. Nevertheless, he still refused to disclose the name of Tsai's supervisor. He maintained that this was a matter of principle for the college and a matter of respect for academia. However, the reality was that the Taiwanese Presidential Office provided the information, and Wilson did not want to respond rashly without confirming the facts

Shih expressed dissatisfaction with this approach. She wished that LSE would remove any suggestion from its initial statement that it did not receive the thesis. Shih believed that this constitutes unfair treatment of Tsai. She also advised LSE to supplement their statement with a refusal to answer external queries on the grounds of data protection law.

The senior ranks at LSE decided to consult with the investigator from 2015, Simeon Underwood, the then LSE's Academic Registrar and Director of Academic Services. Underwood indicated that the documents he saw appeared to be complete. However, he was unsure if any "operation" was involved or even if there was the possibility of forgery.

Underwood's reasoning was straightforward: he only saw photocopies, not the original documents. This situation plunged LSE into an unprecedented predicament.

| | |
|---|---|
| To: | ▮ |
| Date: | 12 June 2019 17:08:17 |
| Attachments: | image002.png |
| | image003.png |
| | image005.png |

Dear ▮,

Thank you for your correspondence, I have been asked to respond with some more information.

Further to your remarks, the records of both the London School of Economics and Political Science and the University of London confirm that Tsai Ing-Wen was awarded a PhD in Law 1984. For your interest, I have attached a scan of a relevant entry in the 'LSE Calendar' of 1985/86, which is an official public record of awards and degrees given to LSE students for the previous year.

The student record shows that the thesis was submitted but the supervisor copy that should have come to LSE Library (the British Library of Political and Economic Science) never did.

As previously circulated, all PhDs from that period were awarded under the University of London banner and would have been sent first to their Senate House Library. They clearly received their copy because otherwise it could not have been catalogued and appear on their catalogue – and from there to the British Library catalogue.

We have been in correspondence with the University of London about the thesis and extensive checks have been made. Senate House are presently unable to find their copy.

I am in touch with colleagues regarding the other pieces of information requested. However, some of them may be restricted by UK data protection laws.


Daniel O'Connor
**Head of Media Relations | Communications Division**
The London School of Economics and Political Science
Houghton Street, London WC2A 2AE
t: +44 (0)20 7955 7417
e: oconnord@lse.ac.uk
**lse.ac.uk**

THE LONDON SCHOOL OF ECONOMICS AND POLITICAL SCIENCE

**LSE is ranked #1 in Europe for social sciences
(QS World University Ranking 2018)**

# RE_For your modification re my draft

**To:** Wilson,Clive; Kelloway,C
**Cc:** Metcalfe,F
**Subject:** RE: For your modification re my draft
**Date:** 12 June 2019 16:32:48

**From:** Shih,F
**Sent:** 12 June 2019 15:16
**To:** Wilson,Clive <CLIVE.Wilson@lse.ac.uk>; Kelloway,C <C.Kelloway@lse.ac.uk>
**Cc:** O'Connor,D <D.O'Connor@lse.ac.uk>; Metcalfe,F <F.Metcalfe@lse.ac.uk>
**Subject:** For your modification re my draft

Dear Clive and Charlotte,

Thank you very much for all your efforts in preparing this LSE press release.

This is very important for alumna President Tsai Ing-wen and the school's reputation as they have been under the irrational attack by anti-Tsai camp during the nomination election in her own political party – DDP.

To be brief, the anti-Tsai's camp includes:

(1)   Taiwanese nationalists (who is against Tsai's policy beyond Chinese and Taiwanese nationalisms toward democracy);

(2)   Taiwanese Independence fundamentalists (who is against Tsai's policy in maintaining the status quo with China);

(3)   Church members (who is against Tsai's government which has recently passed same-sex marriage law)

It is hoped you and the school could understand the current fragile situation and support our alumna and her lead of Taiwan's democracy to the next step as well as to redress the damages to President Tsai and the LSE done by anti-Tsai camp.

The draft letter is fine but is it possible to cut it shorter and add a response to the question of her supervisor and viva examiners?

If this sentence -- "Unfortunately, the LSE Library has never held a copy of Tsai Ing-wen's thesis"— has appeared again, the anti-Tsai camp will continue to attack Tsai, saying she has never submitted her thesis, no matter how many reasons in explaining this. As such, the rest of the sentences regarding her thesis is better not to repeat again (already said in Ruth Orson's 2 emails which have invited the conspiracy to accuse her deceiving of her doctoral degree).

As such, it is hoped you will agree this modified version and please see below:

If not, we also understand the school's concern. Many thanks!

---------------------------------------

An LSE spokesperson said:

"University of London and LSE records confirm Tsai Ing-wen was awarded a PhD in Law in 1984. The LSE has all information, such as the names of Tsai's supervisor and viva examiners. But due to the private data protection, the LSE is unable to release this information without the consent of the individuals. Nevertheless, it is not an unusual case as the supervisor name wasn't always included in the thesis in those days."

----------------------------------------

All the very best,
Fang-long

# RE_ In confidence

| From: | Thomson,MT |
|---|---|
| To: | "Simeon Underwood" |
| Subject: | RE: In confidence |
| Date: | 25 June 2019 09:11:53 |
| Attachments: | image002.png |
| | image003.png |
| | image005.png |
| | image006.png |
| Sensitivity: | Confidential |

Thanks Simeon, that all tallies with what I can make out. I have no doubt that the award was made in line with UoL requirements at the time; and I think there is enough to show that the thesis made its way to Senate House (i.e. because there is a record of it being catalogued), but seems to have been lost when they forwarded it to the Institute for Advanced Legal Studies.

Lots of noise and heat around this one, re: influential LSE alumna, Taiwanese election, political opponents, etc. The play here is to follow regulations and not make any allowances we wouldn't make for any of our graduates.

You may get back to your retirement now.

All best,

MTT

**From:** Simeon Underwood [mailto:simeon.underwood@outlook.com]
**Sent:** 25 June 2019 09:05
**To:** Thomson,MT <M.T.Thomson@lse.ac.uk>
**Subject:** Re: In confidence
**Sensitivity:** Confidential

Mark

I have a vague memory of this. My recollection is that it was no big deal. I got the student file from the archive, and then liaised with Senate House (I am not sure whether Susan Johnson had left by that time). All the paperwork was in order -- by contrast to some files I had seen, notably the senior New Zealand civil servant whose claim to have a PhD turned out to be unprovable and possibly fraudulent. I am not sure there are any "workings". If you are in need of anything further, though, I can have a go at looking further, but without much expectation of finding anything. On the missing thesis, I suspect that this is down to Senate House, the Library or both.

Does that help ?

Simeon

恶官 3

# The Genesis of the Storm: A Photocopy of the 1985/86 Academic Regulations

# The Genesis of the Storm: A Photocopy of the 1985/86 Academic Regulations

The focal point of the storm that is the academic controversy at the LSE is a document known as a photocopy of the academic regulations for the years 1985 and 1986. To the outside world, this document was the sole evidence affirming the proper award of a particular scholar's degree. Yet, for those within the institution, the backstory of this document was much more complex than what met the eye.

O'Connor was persistently in search of substantial evidence that could verify the correct conferral of the degree. However, he encountered a predicament. Back in 2015, the school had stated that the lists of viva examiners and supervising professors could not be disclosed without their consent due to privacy concerns involving the academics. This photocopy of the 85/86 academic regulations was the only evidence he could present. Despite his admission that this document could not serve as concrete evidence, he declared it publicly as proof.

Cerny had a different perspective. He believed the institution should abandon the controversy and stand by this alumna. Cerny repeatedly referenced the findings of the 2015 investigation in attempts to parry external skepticism. Even though he was aware of the numerous doubts surrounding the investigation's results, he was reluctant to delve further, suggesting that the photocopy of the academic regulations from 1985 and 1986 could be used as corroborating evidence to confirm the scholar's possession of the degree.

Shih expressed dissatisfaction with this approach. She arranged a meeting with Wilson and a senior official from the college. Yet, before the meeting, she suddenly stopped responding to any correspondence. This anticipated encounter seemed poised to become the key to unraveling the truth behind this academic dispute.

# Re_Ing-Wen Tsai's Ph.D. thesis (4)

**From:** Orson,R
**To:** Wilson,Clive; O'Connor,D
**Cc:** Cerny,MW; Metcalfe,F; Kelloway,C
**Subject:** Re: Ing Wen Tsai's PhD thesis
**Date:** 11 June 2019 22:08:25

I will not be in the office tomorrow but I would like to know what Nicola and Martin's response to this situation is as soon as possible tomorrow morning.

Ruth Orson
Library Assistant, Research Support Services | LSE Research Online
London School of Economics and Political Science
10 Portugal Street, London WC2A 2HD
tel: 020 7955 3528 | email: R.Orson@lse.ac.uk

**From:** Wilson,Clive
**Sent:** 11 June 2019 20:04:42
**To:** O'Connor,D
**Cc:** Cerny,MW; Metcalfe,F; Kelloway,C; Graham1,N; Orson,R; Lsethesesonline
**Subject:** Re: Ing Wen Tsai's PhD thesis

I've just sent two very polite holding replies although Professor ■■■ chasing is bordering on the rude – although I do appreciate how important the issue is.

Dr Shih is going to come in to see me in the morning at 10. I'll leave a proper reply to the emails until I have spoken to her – but of course happy for anyone to join us.

Clive


**From:** O'Connor,D
**Sent:** 11 June 2019 19:54
**To:** Wilson,Clive
**Cc:** Cerny,MW; Metcalfe,F; Kelloway,C; Graham1,N; Orson,R; Lsethesesonline
**Subject:** Re: Ing-Wen Tsai's PhD thesis

Thanks for this, Clive. Useful to know.

Ruth do forward on any further letters and we can collate and reply from central LSE accounts

Danny

On 11 Jun 2019, at 17:39, Wilson,Clive <CLIVE.Wilson@lse.ac.uk> wrote:

> Hi All
>
> Just had a chat with Dr Fang-Long Shih in the LSE Taiwan Research Programme who is a supporter of Dr Tsai.
>
> Apparently the Taiwan press and the opposition party are trying to relate this to the incident over Saif gaddafi and the Libyan donation.

Supporters of Dr Tsai are therefore very keen to be able to prove that the degree was awarded correctly/successfully and may be able to get permission from Dr Tsai to release more information from her record as appropriate.

And the Calendar is a public document that anyone from outside LSE can request to view through our archives so there is no DP/GDPR issue.

Clive

**From:** Cerny,MW
**Sent:** 11 June 2019 17:15
**To:** O'Connor,D; Metcalfe,F; Kelloway,C; Wilson,Clive; Graham1,N; Orson,R
**Cc:** Lsethesesonline
**Subject:** RE: Ing-Wen Tsai's PhD thesis

My opinion is we should leave it in. We should look like we're pretending to have had nothing to do with this and she is an LSE alumnus (we trumpeted as much ourselves when she got elected).

Thanks,
Marcus

**Marcus Cerny**
*Deputy Director, PhD Academy*
*London School of Economics and Political Science*
*Houghton Street*
*London WC2A 2AE*

Please consider the environment and do not print this email unless absolutely necessary.
Please access the attached hyperlink for an important electronic communications disclaimer:
http://lse.ac.uk/emailDisclaimer

**From:** O'Connor,D
**Sent:** 11 June 2019 17:09
**To:** Metcalfe,F; Kelloway,C; Wilson,Clive; Graham1,N; Cerny,MW; Orson,R
**Cc:** Lsethesesonline
**Subject:** RE: Ing-Wen Tsai's PhD thesis

Thanks. As we're sharing one of LSE's records (the Calendar) I think we should probably leave it in.

(Can switch it around to 'UoL and LSE' though).

D

**From:** Metcalfe,F
**Sent:** 11 June 2019 17:07
**To:** Kelloway,C <C.Kelloway@lse.ac.uk>; O'Connor,D <D.O'Connor@lse.ac.uk>; Wilson,Clive <CLIVE.Wilson@lse.ac.uk>; Graham1,N <N.Graham1@lse.ac.uk>; Cerny,MW

<M.W.Cerny@lse.ac.uk>; Orson,R <R.Orson@lse.ac.uk>
**Cc:** Lsethesesonline <Lsethesesonline@lse.ac.uk>
**Subject:** Re: Ing-Wen Tsai's PhD thesis

Looks good to me. You could lose LSE from the first line putting the ownership firmly in UoL court but is that overkill?

Get Outlook for iOS

**From:** Kelloway,C <c.kelloway@lse.ac.uk>
**Sent:** Tuesday, June 11, 2019 4:49 PM
**To:** O'Connor,D; Wilson,Clive; Graham1,N; Cerny,MW; Orson,R
**Cc:** Lsethesesonline; Metcalfe,F
**Subject:** RE: Ing-Wen Tsai's PhD thesis

Hi all,

We have put together a reply to Hwan and a media statement for any press requests we get about this. Please find these below.

We can send the reply to ▮▮▮▮ (with the library copied in) as it seems this story is starting to spread into the media from sources such as Hwan.

Just one question on the scan of the calendar – does anyone know if sharing this document with external parties will raise any data protection/GDPR issues?

**Letter:**
Dear ▮▮▮▮,

Thank you for your correspondence, I have been asked to respond with some more information.

Further to your remarks, the records of both the London School of Economics and Political Science and the University of London confirm that Tsai Ing-Wen was awarded a PhD in Law 1984. For your interest, I have attached a scan of a relevant entry in the 'LSE Calendar' of 1985/86, which is an official public record of awards and degrees given to LSE students for the previous year.

Unfortunately, the LSE Library has never held a copy of Tsai Ing-wen's thesis. All PhDs from that period were awarded under the University of London banner and would have been sent first to their Senate House Library.

We have been in correspondence with the University of London about the thesis and extensive checks have been made. Senate House are presently unable to find their copy.

[Given these circumstances, it may be worth contacting Dr Tsai's office for detail of the thesis, if she still has a copy]. [optional?]

Kind regards

**Media Statement:**

**An LSE spokesperson said:**

"LSE and University of London records confirm Tsai Ing-wen was awarded a PhD in Law in 1984.

"Unfortunately, the LSE Library has never held a copy of Tsai Ing-wen's thesis. All PhDs from that period were awarded via the University of London and would have been sent first to their Senate House Library.

"We have corresponded with the University of London about the thesis and extensive checks have been made. Senate House Library are presently unable to find their copy."

/END

**As background**
I have attached a scan of the relevant entry in the LSE Calendar of 1985/86, which acts an official record of awards and degrees given to LSE students in 1984.


Many thanks,
Charlotte


**Charlotte Kelloway**
**Media Relations Officer | Communications Division**
The London School of Economics and Political Science
Houghton Street, London WC2A 2AE
t: +44 (0)20 7955 6558
e: c.kelloway@lse.ac.uk
lse.ac.uk

<image001.jpg>

<image002.png><image003.png><image004.jpg><image005.png><image006.jpg>

**LSE is ranked #2 in the world for social science and management.
(QS World University Ranking 2018)**




**From:** O'Connor,D
**Sent:** 11 June 2019 15:20
**To:** Wilson,Clive; Graham1,N; Cerny,MW; Orson,R
**Cc:** Lsethesesonline; Metcalfe,F; Kelloway,C
**Subject:** RE: Ing-Wen Tsai's PhD thesis

Thanks for this Clive.

We're just putting together a version of the response for press/ other external parties.

Separately, we will also retrieve a scan of the relevant 1985/86 calendar page. It's not exactly a smoking gun but might be useful if we start getting more hassle for proof.

I'll ask the School Secretary's office in the first instance…as I imagine they have them to hand.

Thanks,

Danny

**From:** Wilson,Clive
**Sent:** 11 June 2019 15:11
**To:** Graham1,N <N.Graham1@lse.ac.uk>; Cerny,MW <M.W.Cerny@lse.ac.uk>; Orson,R <R.Orson@lse.ac.uk>
**Cc:** O'Connor,D <D.O'Connor@lse.ac.uk>; Lsethesesonline <Lsethesesonline@lse.ac.uk>
**Subject:** RE: Ing-Wen Tsai's PhD thesis

Hi All

yes, I dealt with this for the Library first time around.

Simeon Underwood who was Academic Registrar at the time had the student record retrieved and stated he was satisfied that the degree was correctly awarded (copied below)

It was also decided that all information relating to supervisor, thesis committee and the oral defense committee, etc could not be released without Dr. Tsai's permission.

Nancy's copied our standard reply below, which I have already tweaked slightly to make current. Simeon's instruction also was that anyone pursuing further should be referred to Lorraine. I believe Mark Thomson was also happy with this approach (as he took over directly from Simeon)

happy to try to answer any further questions about what we did if I can.

Clive

Clive Wilson
Enquiry Services Manager (Academic Services)
London School of Economics        Tel.:    020 7955 7475
10 Portugal Street                Fax.:    020 7955 7454
London WC2A 2HD                   Email:   Datalibrary@lse.ac.uk
                                           clive.wilson@lse.ac.uk

# RE_-Ing-Wen-Tsais-PhD-thesis

**From:** O'Connor,D
**Sent:** 11 June 2019 15:20
**To:** Wilson,Clive; Graham1,N; Cerny,MW; Orson,R
**Cc:** Lsethesesonline; Metcalfe,F; Kelloway,C
**Subject:** RE: Ing-Wen Tsai's PhD thesis

Thanks for this Clive.

We're just putting together a version of the response for press/ other external parties.

Separately, we will also retrieve a scan of the relevant 1985/86 calendar page. It's not exactly a smoking gun but might be useful if we start getting more hassle for proof.

I'll ask the School Secretary's office in the first instance…as I imagine they have them to hand.

Thanks,

Danny

**From:** Wilson,Clive
**Sent:** 11 June 2019 15:11
**To:** Graham1,N <N.Graham1@lse.ac.uk>; Cerny,MW <M.W.Cerny@lse.ac.uk>; Orson,R <R.Orson@lse.ac.uk>
**Cc:** O'Connor,D <D.O'Connor@lse.ac.uk>; Lsethesesonline <Lsethesesonline@lse.ac.uk>
**Subject:** RE: Ing-Wen Tsai's PhD thesis

Hi All

yes, I dealt with this for the Library first time around.

Simeon Underwood who was Academic Registrar at the time had the student record retrieved and stated he was satisfied that the degree was correctly awarded (copied below)

It was also decided that all information relating to supervisor, thesis committee and the oral defense committee, etc could not be released without Dr Tsai's permission.

Nancy's copied our standard reply below, which I have already tweaked slightly to make current. Simeon's instruction also was that anyone pursuing further should be referred to Lorraine. I believe Mark Thomson was also happy with this approach (as he took over directly from Simeon)

**From:** Cerny,MW
**Sent:** 11 June 2019 17:15
**To:** O'Connor,D; Metcalfe,F; Kelloway,C; Wilson,Clive; Graham1,N; Orson,R
**Cc:** Lsethesesonline
**Subject:** RE: Ing-Wen Tsai's PhD thesis

My opinion is we should leave it in. We should look like we're pretending to have had nothing to do with this and she is an LSE alumnus (we trumpeted as much ourselves when she got elected).

Thanks,
Marcus

***Marcus Cerny***
*Deputy Director, PhD Academy*

*London School of Economics and Political Science*
*Houghton Street*
*London WC2A 2AE*

**Please consider the environment and do not print this email unless absolutely necessary.**
Please access the attached hyperlink for an important electronic communications disclaimer: http://lse.ac.uk/emailDisclaimer

**From:** O'Connor,D
**Sent:** 11 June 2019 19:54
**To:** Wilson,Clive
**Cc:** Cerny,MW; Metcalfe,F; Kelloway,C; Graham1,N; Orson,R; Lsethesesonline
**Subject:** Re: Ing-Wen Tsai's PhD thesis

Thanks for this, Clive. Useful to know.

Ruth do forward on any further letters and we can collate and reply from central LSE accounts

Danny

On 11 Jun 2019, at 17:39, Wilson,Clive <CLIVE.Wilson@lse.ac.uk> wrote:

> Hi All
>
> Just had a chat with Dr Fang-Long Shih in the LSE Taiwan Research Programme who is a supporter of Dr Tsai.
>
> Apparently the Taiwan press and the opposition party are trying to relate this to the incident over Saif gaddafi and the Libyan donation.

Supporters of Dr Tsai are therefore very keen to be able to prove that the degree was awarded correctly/successfully and may be able to get permission from Dr Tsai to release more information from her record as appropriate.

And the Calendar is a public document that anyone from outside LSE can request to view through our archives so there is no DP/GDPR issue.

Clive

# RE_ FOI query - thesis supervisor

**From:** O'Connor,D
**To:** Wilson,Clive; Maguire,RE
**Subject:** RE: FOI query - thesis supervisor
**Date:** 27 June 2019 14:23:00

I'm happy that we can say something like, "following data protection guidelines we do not, as standard, release the names of PhD supervisors."

It is our default policy, after all.

Danny

**From:** Wilson,Clive
**Sent:** 27 June 2019 14:12
**To:** Maguire,RE <R.E.Maguire@lse.ac.uk>
**Cc:** O'Connor,D <D.O'Connor@lse.ac.uk>
**Subject:** RE: FOI query - thesis supervisor

Thanks Rachael, much appreciated.

I can't help think this journalist will just find it very convenient that the supervisor has died. But although we could release it – we don't have to. It's only really chance that I know that he passed away. Danny – your call on that one ☺

thanks again

Clive

**From:** Maguire,RE
**Sent:** 27 June 2019 14:04
**To:** Wilson,Clive
**Cc:** O'Connor,D
**Subject:** RE: FOI query - thesis supervisor

Hello Clive,

This is not true as this is third party personal information which is being requested. Section 40 of the Freedom of Information Act requires that we consider whether the data protection principles will be breached if we release personal data. The personal data in this case is:

- The degree granted
- The supervisor's name.

The main data protection principle is the first, relating to fairness. We have to consider if it will be fair to release personal data relating to another individual. Regarding the degree, this is fair to release as it is usually in the student's interests to confirm they received the degree they are saying they received. There will be negative consequences for them if we don't. Regarding the supervisor's name, this would not normally be fair because the School does not release the names of teaching staff on a regular basis and there would be an expectation from staff that their names were not released. However, as the supervisor is dead, data protection no longer applies. You have to be a living individual. So the supervisor's name in this instance could be released.

FoI is not a complete right to information anyway, there are exemptions and other reasons we can refuse e.g. vexatious requests. I suggest linking to the ICO's website for more information www.ico.org.uk as a further resource.

Regards,
Rachael

**From:** Wilson,Clive
**Sent:** 27 June 2019 13:52
**To:** Maguire,RE <R.E.Maguire@lse.ac.uk>
**Cc:** O'Connor,D <D.O'Connor@lse.ac.uk>
**Subject:** FOI query - thesis supervisor

Hi Rachel

sorry, more on the Ing-Wen Tsai thesis.

A Chinese journalist has been writing on the disappearance of Ing-Wen Tsai's thesis. I had initially replied to him with our standard response and told him that releasing the supervisor's name was not allowed under UK data protection rules – as Simeon Underwood had stated 4 years ago.

The journalist has come back with

> I consulted a British writer and checked with The Freedom of Information Act of UK, it came to my knowledge that as a public figure, a government official, and let alone a sitting president of a democratic country, any information regarding Ms.Tsai's degree, her thesis, her supervisor, etc. should be public information and LSE is responsible to provide whatever they have.

(I haven't included the long non-LSE related bumpf)

The supervisor passed away in 2016 and hadn't been at LSE since 1984. I feel as though, if he were alive, we would need his permission to release his name. But as Ing-Wen Tsai is the current president of Taiwan do we need to release this?

(I also see there is an international relations exclusion but that's probably a stretch)

Many thanks

Clive

Clive Wilson
Enquiry Services Manager (Academic Services)
London School of Economics     Tel.:    020 7955 7475

惡官 3

## The Strategy of Balancing Between LSE and the Taiwan Presidential Office

# The Strategy of Balancing Between LSE and the Taiwan Presidential Office

Wilson flipped through two hard copies of a thesis sent from the Taiwan Presidential Office. He negotiated with Tsai's team, hoping for a win-win solution.

O'Connor also harbored concerns about the thesis, which was published only in 2019, as this could lead to further questions and controversy. He sought a way to quell the external queries.

Cerny had a more definitive perspective. He believed that the institution should acknowledge the degree awarding process of that year but maintain neutrality regarding whether this thesis was the qualifying work at the time, neither confirming nor denying it. He thought this approach could protect the institution's reputation while not alienating the Taiwan Presidential Office.

After hearing Cerny's suggestion, Wilson mused, "If our library lacked a catalog entry for this thesis, but the author's family provided a copy, I'd bite their hand off for it."

The institution finally settled on a third version of its public statement after a series of investigations and discussions. This statement attempted to balance the institution's reputation with the demands of the Taiwan Presidential Office, but whether it would appease public skepticism remained an open question.

# RE_ More on the Ph.D. Thesis by Ing-Wen Tsai

**From:** O'Connor,D
**Sent:** 28 June 2019 13:27
**To:** Wilson,Clive; Thomson,MT; Kelloway,C; Cerny,MW; Metcalfe,F
**Subject:** RE: More on the PhD Thesis by Ing-Wen Tsai …

Hi Clive,

In normal circumstances, this all sounds very sensible.

However, as Marcus highlighted at the meeting, would we do the same if it were from a run-of-the-mill PhD graduate from the 1980s?

Also, I have a feeling announcing that we now have a facsimile copy might lead to a more confused message and a run of questions, such as : 'can you say it's genuine?' 'If not, are you *refusing* to endorse it?' "It says 2019, are you saying she only just wrote this?" etc. Answerable but may get us in the weeds.

Not saying we shouldn't go with the suggestion, it sounds like a good compromise, but just want to make sure our messaging is in order.

Hope that makes sense. Thanks very much,

Danny


**From:** Wilson,Clive
**Sent:** 28 June 2019 12:11
**To:** Thomson,MT <M.T.Thomson@lse.ac.uk>; Kelloway,C <C.Kelloway@lse.ac.uk>; O'Connor,D <D.O'Connor@lse.ac.uk>; Cerny,MW <M.W.Cerny@lse.ac.uk>; Metcalfe,F <F.Metcalfe@lse.ac.uk>
**Subject:** More on the PhD Thesis by Ing-Wen Tsai …

Hi everyone

I received two copies of the thesis from Taiwan late yesterday. One soft bound and one hard bound. But both photocopies.

There are two draft chapters and an outline on the student record and – in my humble opinion - there is enough of those in the thesis to suggest it is good. And besides, even with the whole wheel of government behind you, it would still be a rather neat trick to fake or rewrite a thesis as if it was done in 1983 and in the same font as the draft chapters. ☺ However, as Marcus said on Monday, we still can't really prove that this is what she actually submitted in 1983.

One of my cataloguing colleagues has said we can probably catalogue it as a facsimile. For example:

Tsai, Ing-Wen. Unfair trade practices and safeguard actions: a facsimile copy of her 1983 PhD thesis presented to LSE Library by President Ing-Wen Tsai of Taiwan. 2019

This makes it clear it's a copy and was presented to us by her – so some deniability on our part if necessary.
By saying it was presented (again) and addressing her as President – it shows we are proud and still claiming brownie points for her as an LSE alumna.
The date shows as 2019 because that's when the copy was made – so again, not claiming it is the actual thesis.

To me, that sounds like a win-win for us and for her team. But happy to take it under advisement.

And then, as previously, we don't have permission to digitise it so it would only be available in the special collections reading room where we have two people at all times who can monitor any copying or defacing. And I would suggest we only give out the soft copy.

How does that sound?

Clive


Marcus in the PhD Academy is concerned that, although it almost certainly is valid, we can't prove that this is what she submitted in 1983. There are two draft chapters and an outline on the student record and there is enough of those in the copy to suggest it is good. And besides, even with the whole wheel of government behind you, it would be a rather neat trick to fake or rewrite a thesis as if it was done in 1983.


Clare said she needed to check but we could catalogue it as a facsimile. Marcus will (probably) be happy provided we make it clear (or ambiguous even) that we are not claiming it's the actual thesis.

So I am thinking something like:

Tsai, Ing-Wen. Unfair trade practices and safeguard actions: a facsimile copy of her 1983 PhD thesis presented to LSE Library by President Ing-Wen Tsai of Taiwan. 2019

If we make it available it would have to be reading room only. Can we restrict copying? Would we still hold it with the print theses? Would we add it to Theses Online even if it isn't digitised?

**The biggest degree fraud case in human history**

**From:** Cerny,MW
**Sent:** 28 June 2019 14:09
**To:** O'Connor,D; Wilson,Clive; Thomson,MT; Kelloway,C; Metcalfe,F
**Subject:** RE: More on the PhD Thesis by Ing-Wen Tsai ...

I am happy with this being available in the library. I can see that it as we have it, and it is of interest, it should be available where possible and my view is also that it is up to the Library to decide whether to accept materials and whether to store and make them available within whatever rules/conditions apply.

However, my decision from a regulatory standpoint, is that this has to be on the basis that this is a document provided to the Library in 2019 and be clear that we are not storing this as a formal record of the thesis examined or awarded.

What wording on the catalogue that might cover this and pre-empt questions is debatable but I think Clive's formulation is a reasonable one. Even if we got the question about it being genuine or whether we endorse it can we not simply fall back on the agreed statement? Noting again that we are satisfied that the thesis was correctly awarded in line with the relevant procedures, that Senate House sent a copy to IALS, that neither Senate House nor IALS can locate a copy, and that Dr Tsai's office provided this version in 2019.

One final note on my position on this. It is not just a question as to whether we can prove that this is the thesis or whether we believe it to be. It is also a question that we would not accept a copy at this late remove in these circumstances for any other candidate and then record it as the examined or awarded thesis. Given this, for purposes of consistency, I do not think we should do so because of an individual graduates status. For the record, I am actually satisfied that this is an accurate version of the thesis examined (but I obviously could not prove it).

Thanks,
Marcus

**Marcus Cerny**
*Deputy Director, PhD Academy*
*London School of Economics and Political Science*
*Houghton Street*

*London WC2A 2AE*

Please consider the environment and do not print this email unless absolutely necessary.
Please access the attached hyperlink for an important electronic communications disclaimer:
http://lse.ac.uk/emailDisclaimer

| | |
|---|---|
| From: | Wilson,Clive |
| To: | Cerny,MW; O"Connor,D; Thomson,MT; Kelloway,C; Metcalfe,F |
| Subject: | RE: More on the PhD Thesis by Ing-Wen Tsai … |
| Date: | 28 June 2019 16:12:03 |
| Attachments: | ▇▇▇▇▇▇▇▇ |

Thanks Marcus

As a librarian I know my view is slightly coloured 😊 . But we can add notes to the record as well as purely bibliographic info, so I will see if I can come up with better wording to make it clearer.

And I know I told Marcus this already but this might also be helpful - I've copied here an email from three of our accounting faculty.

Some LSE Master's dissertations in the first half of last century were done by research. As a result they went to Senate House like the PhDs did.

When PhD theses were repatriated to LSE, the lists did not include the Master's dissertations. As a result most of those dissertations have been scrapped but the Senate House catalogue points to us.

Some of those dissertations are very heavily cited – so from a purely academic perspective are far more important - but if we did not have a duplicate they are lost. I find this heartbreaking. We get five or six enquiries a year about these. I would suspect all of those authors are dead now, but if a family member was doing some research and said, it's not on your catalogue but I have a copy – I'd bite their hand off!!

Clive

**From:** Kelloway,C
**Sent:** 28 June 2019 16:37
**To:** Wilson,Clive; Cerny,MW; O'Connor,D; Thomson,MT; Metcalfe,F
**Subject:** RE: More on the PhD Thesis by Ing-Wen Tsai …

Hi all,

I have added a line to the statement to reflect this new development. Let me know if you would like to make any edits.

I've tried to make it clear that the document was only recently provided to us and that we are not storing it as a formal record of the thesis but let me know if you think this isn't clear enough.

**LSE spokesperson:**

"The records of the University of London and London School of Economics and Political Science confirm Tsai Ing-Wen was correctly awarded a PhD in Law in 1984.

"All PhDs from that period were awarded via the University of London and would have been sent first to their Senate House Library. It is clear from Senate House Library records that a copy was received. Senate House have confirmed they sent their copy of the thesis to the Institute for Advanced Legal Studies (IALS).

"We have corresponded with the University of London about the thesis and extensive checks have been made. Neither Senate House nor IALS are able to locate a copy of the thesis.

"President Tsai Ing-wen's office recently provided the LSE Library with a facsimile copy of the thesis, *Unfair trade practices and safeguard actions*. This is available to view in the library's reading room."

/END

**As background**
I have attached a scan of the relevant entry in the LSE Calendar of 1985/86, which acts an official record of awards and degrees given to LSE students in 1984. This confirms Dr Tsai's PhD award at the time.

General response:

Thank you for your email. We have checked our records and both the London School of Economics and Political Science and the University of London confirm that Tsai Ing Wen was correctly awarded a PhD in Law 1984.

However, all PhDs from that period were awarded via the University of London and would have been sent first to their Senate House Library. It is clear from Senate House Library records that a copy was received. Senate House have confirmed they sent their copy of the thesis to the Institute for Advanced Legal Studies (IALS).

We have corresponded with the University of London about the thesis and extensive checks have been made. Neither Senate House nor IALS are able to locate a copy of the thesis,

However, President Tsai Ing wen's office recently provided the LSE Library with a facsimile copy of the thesis, *Unfair trade practices and safeguard actions*. This is available to view in the library's reading room.

Many thanks,
Charlotte

恶官 ₃

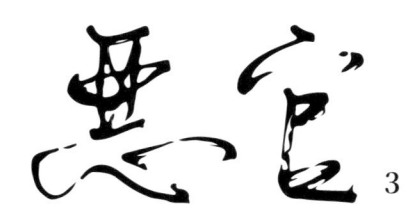

# Confidential Instructions: Internal Struggle at the University of London

# Confidential Instructions: Internal Struggle at the University of London

Within the internal documents and records of the LSE, the examiner's name for a particular student's viva appears to have vanished, with even the name of the thesis advisor becoming a mystery. This student was none other than Tsai, who would later become the President of Taiwan.

In 2015, as the controversy over Tsai's academic credentials intensified in the Taiwanese media, actions were already being taken within LSE. An anonymous insider at the University of London had begun issuing instructions on how the college should respond to the dispute. Everything was handled with a high level of secrecy, known only to a select few.

Underwood parried many inquiries with falsehoods. He understood that the controversy was not just about academic truth but was entwined with political maneuvering. Behind him stood Mark Thomson and Wilson, staff members of the LSE Academic Registry Department, who were central figures involved in this controversy since 2015.

Wilson was aware that the college never internalized Tsai's thesis. Yet, he also recognized vast political stakes and machinations behind the controversy. In 2016, when the issue of Tsai's thesis resurfaced, Wilson decided to step back from further involvement. He reasoned that Tsai had been elected President of Taiwan, and the dispute was unlikely to be rekindled.

But the truth always remains the truth. Should the truth be obscured for political gains within the halls of academia? That is a question and a challenge.

# RE_-Need-to-find-a-1984-Ph.D.-dissertation-in-y

**Cc:** Foster,NK
**Subject:** RE: Need to find a 1984 Ph.D. dissertation in your department

Dear Simeon,

Please do pass any enquiries regarding this PhD examination on to me. I can help with some of ▇ questions below if you forward me his email address. As for the actual copies of the thesis itself I am sorry I am unable to shed any light on this. Both examiners' copies of the thesis were left at the LSE following examination. It seems the third copy of the thesis was sent to the IALS, and then the trail goes cold.

We have retrieved Dr Tsai's file from our Archives and I can send you through a scanned copy if that would be useful.

With best wishes,

▇

**UNIVERSITY OF LONDON**

▇ University of London is an exempt charity in England and Wales.
We are committed to achieving a 20% cut in emissions from University buildings by 2015. Please think before you print.

**From:** Underwood,S
**Sent:** 03 July 2015 15:44
**To:** Green,LJ; Yarham,R; Bannister,HR; Foster,NK; Wright,NC; Reid,MJ; Wilson,Clive; Donnelly,S; Thomas4,A; O'Connor,D
**Subject:** FW: Need to find a 1984 Ph.D. dissertation in your department

Colleagues

Herewith correspondence with Senate House about Dr Tsai's PhD examination and thesis. The upshot is that any future correspondence should go to Lorraine at Senate House. But please send them with a copy to me until 20 July and a copy to Louisa Green thereafter, in case there are any issues which are specific to the School.

Many thanks

simeon

**From:** Underwood,S
**Sent:** 03 July 2015 15:40
**To:**
**Cc:** Foster,NK
**Subject:** RE: Need to find a 1984 Ph.D. dissertation in your department

Thanks for this.

The line I have taken is that we can't give ▮▮▮ the answers to his questions for reasons to do with data protection. I wrote to him on Monday; and he hasn't got back to me as yet. I suggest that we let this lie unless he gets back to us. But if you think differently please say.

Thanks for the kind offer, but I will manage with a copy of Dr Tsai's university file, for now at least.

All the best

simeon

The biggest degree fraud case in human history

**Sent:** 10 November 2015 13:32
**To:** Green,LJ; Thomson,MT
**Cc:** Flanagan,D; Reid,MJ
**Subject:** RE: Need to find a 1984 Ph.D. dissertation in your department

Dear Mark

I'm not sure if you are aware of this particular issue or not so my apologies if much of this is known to you.

In brief, one of our alumna Ing-Wen Tsai is her party's candidate in the upcoming Taiwan elections. As the email trail below shows there appears to be no available copy of her PhD thesis although Simeon Underwood was satisfied that the record showed the award was valid.

We have had a number of requests for this thesis since the candidacy was announced and have given a standard response and referred to ██████████ at Senate House as Simeon requested.

I mention it now because it appears to have made the Chinese press in Canada and mentioned on twitter: ████████████████████████████████

████████████████████████████████████████
████████████████████████████████████████
████████████████████████████████████████
████████████████████████████████████████
████████████████████████████████████████
████████████████████████████████████████

It's all fairly low level so far but I thought you should be aware

Best wishes

Clive

Clive Wilson
Enquiry Services Manager (Academic Services)
London School of Economics Tel.: 020 7955 7475
10 Portugal Street Fax.: 020 7955 7454
London WC2A 2HD Email: Datalibrary@lse.ac.uk
clive.wilson@lse.ac.uk

**FOUNDATIONS**
LSE and the Science of Society

The biggest degree fraud case in human history

**Cc:** Flanagan,D; Reid,MJ; Yarham,R
**Subject:** Re: Need to find a 1984 Ph.D. dissertation in your department

Dear Mark

Sue Donnelly would be able to provide a copy of Dr Tsai's LSE student file - I have copied her in.

Simeon said in one email that:
My understanding is that the position seems to be that two copies were left with LSE from the supervisor and the internal examiner but that these were never passed on to SHL and that one copy went from Senate House Library to IALS but can no longer be found.

I am sure this was based on notes in the relevant LSE and UL records

Rachel Yarham in Law - -also copied now - was asked about it at one point but I believe the department had nothing to add.

It all became a series of unfortunate deadends with no trace of a physical copy anywhere.

Clive

---

**From:** Thomson,MT
**Sent:** 12 November 2015 16:34
**To:** Wilson,Clive; Green,LJ
**Cc:** Flanagan,D; Reid,MJ
**Subject:** RE: Need to find a 1984 Ph.D. dissertation in your department

Clive, greetings

Thank you for this note — apologies for the delayed response, but I made the mistake of being away at a conference early in the week and have paid a heavy price in terms of the state of my inbox.

I was not aware of this matter. A couple of questions:

-Does the PhD Academy have a copy of Dr Tsai's student file? If so, may I see it?

-Do we know the basis on which ▓▓▓▓▓▓▓▓, in her email of 3 July 2015, makes the statement that "Both examiners' copies of the thesis were left at the LSE following examination"?

-Do we know who Dr Tsai's supervisor was, and whether she/he is still at the School and might have a copy of the thesis? Have we tried the department?

All best,

MTT

78  The biggest degree fraud case in human history

**From:** Wilson,Clive
**Sent:** 22 March 2016 16:51
**To:** Thomson,MT; Yarham,R; Green,LJ
**Cc:** Flanagan,D; Reid,MJ
**Subject:** RE: Need to find a 1984 Ph.D. dissertation in your department

Dear Mark

Rachel rang me a short while ago to say that a U.S. research student had been digging around at Senate House for more information on Dr Tsai's thesis. As there is nothing further to be uncovered at LSE I suspect that will be it, but again thought I should let you know in case they end up getting through to your office.

We don't appear to have had any further interest via the Library despite Dr Tsai winning the election.

Best wishes

Clive

# The Fog of Time:
# The Entanglement of 1984 and 2011

# The Fog of Time:
# The Entanglement of 1984 and 2011

Cerny faced a perplexing issue: Why was Tsai's doctoral thesis missing from the college's library? Thomson confirmed with Underwood. However, Underwood's response was evasive; he said he could not be sure of any "operations", adding to the issue's complexity.

O'Connor planned to respond to external inquiries with an ambiguous statement: the thesis had been sent to the University of London's Senate House Library. But Cerny knew this incident occurred in 2011, not 1984, and he wrestled with whether to disclose the truth.

The college librarians expressed their confusion and sought guidance from their superiors. Cerny was still determining whether to report the issue, worried about the potential impact on the college's reputation.

Rita, another employee at the college, suggested in an email that she believed Tsai did not hold a degree and recommended notifying the 2015 investigation officer. Displeased with this assertion, O'Connor perceived the situation as a political struggle. He caustically remarked that Professor Lin , who had inquired about the degree, was in league with the Chinese Communist Party.

Cerny decided to report the issue to the college's board, fearing that LSE might take the fall for the University of London. He understood that the controversy was not just about the academic truth but also about political maneuvering. Eventually, Cerny obfuscated the timeline, leading people to mistakenly believe the thesis was submitted in 1984. O'Connor decided to respond with falsehoods to external inquiries, knowing this would overturn the initial statement by Wilson. However, he believed it was necessary to protect the college's reputation.

This narrative's lines between truth and falsehood, politics, and academia, had become disturbingly blurred.

# RE_-Need-to-find-a-1984-Ph.D.-dissertation-in-y

**From:** Cerny,MW
**Sent:** Friday, June 7, 2019 3:37:24 PM
**To:** Metcalfe,F
**Subject:** FW: PhD Thesis by Ing-Wen Tsai

Dear Fiona,

Could you or a member of your team advise on this? I would expect that there may have been queries in other parts of the School following Tsai's election as President of Republic of China and we may get more queries on this.

I am unable to answer as to why the thesis is unavailable and if the thesis is not held in either Senate House or LSE Libraries I cannot see any chance of there being any other version of it elsewhere.

The email trail between the Library and the enquirer is attached.

Thanks,
Marcus

**Marcus Cerny**
*Deputy Director, PhD Academy*
*London School of Economics and Political Science*
*Houghton Street*
*London WC2A 2AE*

Please consider the environment and do not print this email unless absolutely necessary.
Please access the attached hyperlink for an important electronic communications disclaimer
http://lse.ac.uk/emailDisclaimer

**From:** Thomson,MT
**Sent:** 25 June 2019 19:38
**To:** Wilson,Clive; Kelloway,C; O'Connor,D; Cerny,MW; Metcalfe,F
**Subject:** RE: PhD Thesis by Ing-Wen Tsai

Colleagues, greetings

Further to our discussion yesterday, I got in touch with my predecessor – Simeon Underwood – who conducted the review of the file a few years ago that established that the award was made properly.

He had some memory of the case. His review amounted to looking carefully at the archived file. He concluded that all of the paperwork was in order that indicated that the award was made. He didn't have much more to add.

All best,

MTT

# RE_ Response on Ph.D. Thesis by Ing-Wen Tsai

**From:** Cerny,MW
**Sent:** 27 June 2019 13:20
**To:** O'Connor,D <D.O'Connor@lse.ac.uk>; Wilson,Clive <CLIVE.Wilson@lse.ac.uk>
**Cc:** Metcalfe,F <F.Metcalfe@lse.ac.uk>; Kelloway,C <C.Kelloway@lse.ac.uk>
**Subject:** RE: Response on PhD Thesis by Ing-Wen Tsai

If I recall, the thesis was actually sent to IALS in 2011. This makes sense to me because it will have been around the time that the Research Degrees Office shut at UofL and remaining responsibilities were devolved to individual institutions (though LSE had already assumed these). I imagine they will have been clearing up a number of things outstanding around that time.

I would keep the date out of it and just say that Senate House Library confirmed they sent it to IALS. If anybody wants to ask them for details as to what happened and when, then that is for UoL to respond to (or not) as they see fit.

Thanks,
Marcus

**Marcus Cerny**
*Deputy Director, PhD Academy*
*London School of Economics and Political Science*
*Houghton Street*
*London WC2A 2AE*

Please consider the environment and do not print this email unless absolutely necessary.
Please access the attached hyperlink for an important electronic communications disclaimer: http://lse.ac.uk/emailDisclaimer

---

**From:** O'Connor,D
**Sent:** 27 June 2019 13:11
**To:** Wilson,Clive
**Cc:** Cerny,MW; Metcalfe,F; Kelloway,C
**Subject:** Response on PhD Thesis by Ing-Wen Tsai

Hi Clive,

I'm not dead-set on responding to ▇ but, if I were to respond, it might be along the lines below.

I realise he's clinging on to the initial response from you and Ruth, which suggested that LSE and UoL 'never received' a copy. I can indicate that this was an error but do say if you feel this misrepresents you.

(I'm not addressing all the other conspiracy bumf).

Danny

-CC- ing Marcus and colleagues for any other comments

---

**Draft response**

Dear ▇,

The response I gave still stands. All our records indicate the PhD was correctly awarded and in line with relevant procedures.

Unfortunately the thesis (which was only available as a hard copy in 1984) cannot be found by the University of London or the IALS but records do indicate it was received and processed at the time.

You state that Clive Wilson and his colleague said the 'PhD thesis has never been received in 1984 by Senate House Library and IALS library' in their initial response. This information does not appear to be correct, apologies for the confusion.

| | |
|---|---|
| **From:** | Kelloway,C |
| **To:** | Wilson,Clive |
| **Cc:** | Cerny,MW |
| **Subject:** | RE: President Tsai |
| **Date:** | 10 July 2019 14:40:03 |
| **Attachments:** | image002.png |
| | image003.png |
| | image005.png |

Although this news story has just gone online with President Tsai holding the certificate signed by Adrian Smith...

https://www.taiwannews.com.tw/en/news/3742447

**From:** Kelloway,C
**Sent:** 10 July 2019 14:30
**To:** Wilson,Clive
**Cc:** Cerny,MW
**Subject:** RE: President Tsai

Thanks for the detective work on this, Clive – this is good to know!

We'll point them to University of London for questions about degree certificates but, as an aside, will also ask the origins of these certificates.

Many thanks,
Charlotte

**From:** Wilson,Clive
**Sent:** 10 July 2019 13:27
**To:** Cerny,MW; Kelloway,C
**Subject:** RE: President Tsai

I love being a librarian!!!

https://en.wikipedia.org/wiki/List_of_Vice-Chancellors_of_the_University_of_London

It looks to me like that is Adrian Smith's signature on both. University of London VP from 2012 – 2018.

But it was a different signature on the one I sent a few weeks ago ... (attached)   Randolph Quirk was VP in 1984

And UCL have also awarded their own degrees since 2008  and should be on UCL paper and signed by current president and provost Professor Michael Arthur??   And the date isn't straight ...

So the certificate for Ing Wen Tsai is clearly a fake.   And the UCL one is almost certainly a fake.

☺

Clive

**From:** Cerny,MW
**Sent:** 10 July 2019 11:58
**To:** Kelloway,C
**Cc:** Wilson,Clive
**Subject:** RE: President Tsai

Thanks Charlotte,

Definitely for UofL that one. I suspect that they have the signatures on file and use the one that was responsible for verifying the award at the time it was made but I don't know that for sure.

Thanks,
Marcus

**Marcus Cerny**
Deputy Director, PhD Academy
London School of Economics and Political Science
Houghton Street
London WC2A 2AE

Please consider the environment and do not print this email unless absolutely necessary.
Please access the attached hyperlink for an important electronic communications disclaimer:
http://lse.ac.uk/emailDisclaimer

**From:** Kelloway,C
**Sent:** 10 July 2019 11:38
**To:** Cerny,MW
**Cc:** Wilson,Clive
**Subject:** FW: President Tsai

Hi Marcus,

I hope you're well.

We've had the below enquiry from a journalist about President Tsai's PhD. We plan to send the response we have prepared with a note that the thesis will be available to view in the library imminently.

However, she also provides a recent University of London degree certificate and an apparent copy of President Tsai's degree certificate and questions why the Vice Chancellor's signature is the same on both despite the 34 year time difference.

We plan to say this is a question for the University of London but internally wanted to explore why this is the case and were wondering if you had any insight?

We're not sure of the origin of either of the photos.

Many thanks,

Charlotte

**Charlotte Kelloway**
**Media Relations Officer | Communications Division**
The London School of Economics and Political Science
Houghton Street, London WC2A 2AE
t: +44 (0)20 7955 6558
e: c.kelloway@lse.ac.uk
lse.ac.uk

THE LONDON SCHOOL OF ECONOMICS AND POLITICAL SCIENCE

LSE is ranked #2 in the world for social science and management.
(QS World University Ranking 2018)

**From:**
**Sent:** 10 July 2019 06:39
**To:** Events
**Subject:** I would like to check some information from LSE

Here is
There is an issue in Taiwan, it's about President Tsai who got PHD from LSE in 1984. There are some media and people said it's a fake degree, because it couldn't find her Doctoral dissertation.

And each one of host who posted two certification to doubt why President Tsai graduated in 1984, another certification graduated in 2018, but Vise chancellor is same.

Could you please help me to figure out this issue? I'm curious the truth.

I'm apologize to bother you, and looking forward your help and reply.

Best Regard.

88    The biggest degree fraud case in human history

# Note for SMC on Tsai's thesis

| | |
|---|---|
| **From:** | O"Connor,D |
| **To:** | Withers,JF |
| **Cc:** | Metcalfe,F |
| **Subject:** | Note for SMC on Tsai thesis |
| **Date:** | 19 July 2019 11:12:00 |
| **Attachments:** | image002.png |
| | image003.png |
| | image005.png |

Hi,

Laura Ross has asked for a brief note on the Tsai PhD issue to inform SMC.

I've provided a two pager...but probably better this than too little.

Are you ok for me to send?

Thanks,

Danny

## [CONFIDENTIAL]
## Issues relating to President Tsai LSE PhD thesis

### Background
At the time of her election in 2016, LSE received enquiries about the 1984 PhD in Law awarded to President Tsai Ing-wen. Upon review, it was established that neither the LSE library nor the University of London had a copy of the thesis. It appeared the University of London had lost the copy which LSE would have sent to them as standard.

Former Academic Registrar, Simeon Underwood, reviewed her student file at the time and found it to be in order. There was no reason to question the awarding of the thesis. He also indicated that the School should not share detailed information about the thesis, given data protection restrictions.

In 2019, the issue re-emerged as the Taiwan Presidential elections approach. Some activists and opponents of President Tsai, both pro-Beijing and also within her Democratic Party, are questioning the validity of the PhD, given that it cannot be found.

Further enquiries from the LSE Library in 2019 confirmed that the University of London had a record of cataloguing her thesis and sending it to Institute of Advanced Legal Studies, though they also were unable to find a copy.

### The current availability of the thesis
Following a number of enquiries and some public discussion in Taiwan, the LSE Library was contacted by President Tsai's office who offered to send a copy of her PhD to the Library, to be available to view upon request.

Following discussion between representatives from the media relations office, PhD Academy, Library and Registry it was agreed the thesis could be catalogued as a 'facsimile copy provided by Tsai Ing-wen'. (Although there was no reason to believe the thesis would be different to the original 1984 submission we cannot for absolute certain it is the same, as we do not have an original copy to compare).

The thesis has been received and has, as of the week commencing 15 July, been catalogued and made available to view in the library, on request.

**Media and public enquiries**
The LSE Library and others have received a number of enquiries, primarily from members of the public but also from a few Taiwanese journalists.
Initial responses in June 2019 indicated that both the University of London and LSE can confirm the PhD was correctly awarded but that the University of London unfortunately no longer has a copy. A photocopy of the relevant LSE Calendar entry confirming her PhD graduation was attached as further evidence.

Following receipt of the thesis and more information becoming available, the media statement and information for public text has now been updated, as below.

**LSE Statement:**

"The records of the University of London and London School of Economics and Political Science confirm Tsai Ing-Wen was correctly awarded a PhD in Law in 1984.
"All PhDs from that period were awarded via the University of London and would have been sent first to their Senate House Library. It is clear from Senate House Library records that a copy was received. Senate House have confirmed they sent their copy of the thesis to the Institute for Advanced Legal Studies (IALS).
"We have corresponded with the University of London about the thesis and extensive checks have been made. Neither Senate House nor IALS are able to locate a copy of the original thesis.
"Dr Tsai Ing-wen recently provided the LSE Library with a facsimile copy of the thesis, 'Unfair trade practices and safeguard actions'. This is now available to view in the library's reading room."
/END

To note, the library has confirmed LSE would catalogue facsimile copies of any missing thesis where there was substantial interest or numerous requests to view. This is not special treatment because she is President of Taiwan.

**Certificate issue**
Additional questions have been asked regarding the physical certificate President Tsai has been displaying in public meetings. Many critics pointed out that it bears the signature of the *current* Vice Chancellor rather than the VC from 1984 when it would have been awarded.

After consulting the LSE media relations office, The University of London have drafted a statement, to indicate that it is a legitimate certificate (it was re-issued to Tsai Ing-wen in 2015). Their re-issue policy is if that if the individual graduated under 20 years ago the signature of the VC at the time would be on the certificate. If over 20 years ago it would contain the signature of the VC at the time of re-issue.

Their statement is to be signed off imminently. Once this has been confirmed LSE will add it alongside own statement, where relevant, with the following text:

"Questions regarding the PhD certificate itself are a matter for the University of London. They have provided the following statement on this matter:

**Draft statement by University of London (TBC):**
*"The University of London can confirm that the diploma certificate re-issued to Dr Tsai Ing-wen is genuine and is signed by the Vice-Chancellor in post at the time of the diploma certificate being reissued.*
*"Any replacement diploma for an academic award that was originally made 20 or more years ago, will carry the signature of the University of London's Vice-Chancellor, who is in post at the time of the certificate being re-issued."*

**Next steps and ongoing coverage.**
This issue is primarily being led by political opponents of President Tsai and anti-Tsai online activists. It is relatively limited to anti-Tsai media in Taiwan. Given LSE and University of London's firm stance that the PhD was legitimate- and additional evidence, such as the availability of the thesis copy – it is unlikely to break into any mainstream media.

It is likely there will be ongoing enquiries from resolute opponents, who may find any explanation hard to accept. Our recommendation is we stick to agreed statement including,, where relevant, an offer for the individual to view the thesis and the statement by the University of London regarding the certificate itself.

Daniel O'Connor
**Head of Media Relations | Communications Division**
The London School of Economics and Political Science
Houghton Street, London WC2A 2AE
t: +44 (0)20 7955 7417
e: oconnord@lse.ac.uk
lse.ac.uk

THE LONDON SCHOOL OF ECONOMICS AND POLITICAL SCIENCE

**LSE is ranked #1 in Europe for social sciences**
**(QS World University Ranking 2018)**

# RE_ [Academic Support Librarians] purchasing a ....

| From: | Wilson,Clive |
|---|---|
| To: | O"Connor,D |
| Subject: | RE: [Academic Support Librarians] purchasing a copy of Ph. D thesis |
| Date: | 29 July 2019 17:18:28 |

No problem 😊
thanks

**From:** O'Connor,D
**Sent:** 29 July 2019 16:39
**To:** Wilson,Clive
**Subject:** RE: [Academic Support Librarians] purchasing a copy of Ph. D thesis

Hi Clive,

Sorry, I didn't respond on this.

Don't reply with the suggested.

I'd say don't bother replying at all.

Danny

**From:** Wilson,Clive
**Sent:** 25 July 2019 16:31
**To:** O'Connor,D <D.O'Connor@lse.ac.uk>
**Subject:** FW: [Academic Support Librarians] purchasing a copy of Ph. D thesis

Hi Danny

I'll keep my mouth shut in future ...

Trying to think of a way to say we don't have permission to digitise without actually saying we don't have permission ... came up with the following ...

Any better ideas? No particular rush ...
thanks

Clive

### [Internal Note] Clive Wilson

Dear ■

I am not entering into an endless backwards and forwards on this. As both LSE and the University of London have confirmed, Dr. Tsai's PhD was correctly awarded.

Although more recent theses are submitted electronically, older theses specifically need the author's permission to be digitised. If Dr Tsai wishes her thesis to be digitised we will happily do so.

[Queue Transfer from Library Enquiries to Academic Support Librarians]

[Status changed to *Pending*]

---

███████████

Hi Clive,Thanks so much for your response on this matter.
Would you please advise the reason why Mrs.Tsai's thesis is not available from this etheses website?Since your library recently received her personal copy, can we expect her thesis be converted to pdf and open to public for download in the near future?
Thanks.
Jimpo


http://etheses.lse.ac.uk/view/year/1984.html?fbclid=IwAR3HBSoEbY_pawK4ukFzFHYsyJC3fBPk_OD2Tr3EzV97k0a02lfbdgndLP4

---

Clive Wilson

Hi ███

yes, the thesis can be viewed. But as I said, you need the author's permission to have it copied.

Clive

---

███████████

Hi Clive,Thanks for the prompt response to my request.Is this publication open to public at this moment? If yes, can I have someone come to your library to make the copy for me?

---

Clive Wilson

Dear ███

even in the US there are plenty of examples of theses where the author has specifically requested that the thesis is neither online nor copied.

Under UK copyright law, the author's permission needs to be given in order to quote or reproduce any part of a thesis. If you have the author's permission you are welcome to arrange to have it copied, however we do not offer a copying service.

You would also be welcome to visit to view the item.

best wishes

Clive

Clive Wilson
Enquiry Services Manager
LSE Library

## Original Question

**purchasing a copy of Ph. D thesis**
Dear LSE Library Staff,
I am currently doing some research in the area of unfair trading and found some Ph.D thesis interesting to me.
Based on my experience in U.S.A I believe all theses are public and can be purchased at reasonable cost.
Would you please advise the cost and process of acquiring the copy of the following thesis?

Author: Tsai, Ing-Wen
Title: Unfair trade practices and safeguard actions

Best Regards,

## Questioner Information

Name:
Email:

Clive Wilson Enquiry Services LSE Library

This email is sent from LSE Library in relationship to ticket id #2675412.

Read our privacy policy.

惡ङ 3

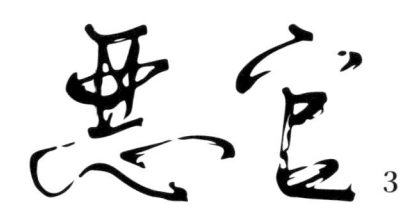

## LSE's Strategy of Ambiguity

## LSE's Strategy of Ambiguity

In London, several top officials at the LSE "raised their glasses" in celebration. They had successfully subdued a potential PR storm that could have caused substantial harm to the institution.

However, the storm had not entirely dissipated. News of Tsai's lawsuit sent shockwaves through their ranks. They had not anticipated such a forceful reaction from the leader of Taiwan. In an internal meeting, one official joked with a hint of sarcasm, "Our testimonies are prepared."

O'Connor, a seasoned public relations expert, suggested that Wilson should employ more ambiguous language when addressing the public. He argued that caution was imperative as Tsai's legal action could escalate the situation. They wanted to avoid becoming the center of media attention once more.

Soon after, representatives from Taiwan's office in the UK visited LSE, seeking confirmation that Tsai's thesis was just one of the ones included. This intensified the anxiety amongst the senior ranks at LSE. They worried that if only Tsai's thesis was missing, it could unravel into a significant scandal. LSE's top officials once again adeptly navigated around such assertions with vague articulations.

On August 27, 2019, Professor Lin released a 50-page "Independent Investigation Report on Tsai's Thesis," directly claiming that Tsai did not receive her Ph.D. in Law from LSE in 1984. Two days later, Professor He hosted a "Presidential Doctoral Thesis Briefing" at the Legislative Yuan, reaching similar conclusions.

The Taiwan Presidential Office responded swiftly. On August 29, spokesperson Chang Tun-Han held a press conference, announcing legal action against Professors Lin and He, deeming their allegations false.

# RE_ [Academic Support Librarians] purchasing a ....

**From:** Cerny,MW
**To:** O"Connor,D; Wilson,Clive
**Subject:** RE: [Library Enquiries] PhD thesis search
**Date:** 09 July 2019 13:33:00

Thanks for keeping me up to date with this. I'm pretty relaxed about this given that there is no question that the thesis existed and was examined. Do people not think that if we were genuinely engaged in a conspiracy we'd have pretty certainly managed to come across a copy that had been misplaced on a shelf in one of the Libraries.

I think that the clarity we are showing in being open about the thesis being lost and the current copy being a recently submitted facsimile replacing the original demonstrates that there is no corruption or cover up.

Once a query becomes a circular correspondence (as one of mine did) I think it's fine to simply ignore after giving the formal response.

Thanks,
Marcus

**Marcus Cerny**
Deputy Director, PhD Academy
London School of Economics and Political Science
Houghton Street
London WC2A 2AE

Please consider the environment and do not print this email unless absolutely necessary.
Please access the attached hyperlink for an important electronic communications disclaimer:
http://lse.ac.uk/emailDisclaimer

**From:** O'Connor,D
**Sent:** 09 July 2019 11:36
**To:** Wilson,Clive; Cerny,MW
**Subject:** Re: [Library Enquiries] PhD thesis search

Thanks Clive.

I would be amazed if the Guardian or NYT followed up with a story beyond a short, 'oops, how embarrassing that they lost her PhD'. If our records say she graduated they should take that as confirmation.

(Separately, "panda huggers" ! )

Danny

**From:** Wilson,Clive

**Sent:** 09 July 2019 11:28:09
**To:** Cerny,MW; O'Connor,D
**Subject:** FW: [Library Enquiries] PhD thesis search

Dear Both

fyi – I'm chasing our making it available right now!.

Clive

**From:** LSE Library [mailto:Library.enquiries@lse-uk.libanswers.com]
**Sent:** 09 July 2019 11:23
**To:** Wilson,Clive
**Subject:** [Library Enquiries] PhD thesis search

--# Please type your reply above this line, it will be sent as a response to the patron #--
A new reply has been submitted for Ticket #2633151 and is awaiting attention. View this ticket at https://lse-uk.libanswers.com/admin/ticket?qid=2633151.

### Hughes,CR
Jul 09 2019, 11:33am via Email

Dear Clive

Thanks so much for this. It is an issue that is being dramatized and distorted for political reasons, so these steps should put the issue to rest.

All the best
Chris

### Clive Wilson
Jul 09 2019, 11:23am via Admin

Dear Both
LSE has made it very clear that the thesis was submitted properly and that the degree could not have been awarded without it. (Some people should just learn how to read.)
I can probably say now that President Tsai has given us two facsimile copies of her thesis which we are trying to rush through to make them available. Due to excessive interest we will not digitise it, though researchers will be very welcome to request it in our Special Collections Reading Room.
best wishes
Clive
Clive Wilson
Enquiry Services Manager
LSE Library

### Hughes,CR
Jul 09 2019, 10:07am via Email

Dear ▓

Thanks for cc'ing me into this. It is incredibly frustrating for everybody, esp Pres Tsai. I guess the simple fact is that things do go missing, and given Tsai's high priority, it is certainly possible that someone or some organization with bad intentions has taken the thesis from the library. The fact that the LSE has recorded her as having been awarded the PhD should be enough to close down any allegations that she did not do one. As for quality, the LSE can only stand by the rigour of its examination procedures. Unless Pres Tsai has a copy of the thesis, then I don't see what anyone can do about this now.

Good to hear from you and keep in touch

Dear Mr. Wilson:
This is ▇▇▇▇▇▇ again. I thought President Tsai's PhD thesis problem had been solved, but it rekindled again, as you may see from the four attached reports and email. It is almost getting out of hand.

The naysayers even use the Guardian report to throw the doubt about the existence and authenticity of Tsai's thesis. See docu #2. I hope this will not happen to Tsai. The best way now seems to me that the LSE finds her thesis committee members to get her thesis and relist/publish it and replace it in the LSE library. (My third book is forthcoming from World Scientific, I even can help her publish it with my commentary).

I think LSE should do something to clarify the thesis ASAP before the Guardian, NYT or Washington Post picks up the news story (it will be a sensational). It seems to me reputation of the LSE is at stake.

PS. I am cc to Professor Chris Hughes.
As for #4 about the English writing of Ma (or Tsai), if this is the concern of LSE, I don't think it should be the concern. As Wassily Leontief, a Harvard Professor and a Nobel Prize winner in Economics, once wrote in the introduction of his book, "American Sciences were advanced by broken English."
In fact, everybody knows two birds are plural, you don't need to add s to show it, or worry about the tense or articles. At least 6 billion of people speak Chinese and Japanese without using plural, tense and articles.

Attached Files
- 0Richardson_British_Library_Richardreversal_on_Tsai_Ing-wen's_phantom_thesis_deepens_mystery_of_missing_manuscript.pdf
- 1Richardson_Tsai_Ing-wen's_missing_thesis_was_not_submitted_says_university_library_-_Richardson_Reports.pdf
- 2Richardson_lttr_to.pdf
- 3Richardson_TIW_official_CV_fm_TGov.pdf
- 4Richardson_Tsai_Ing-wen's_missing_doctoral_thesis_follows_Ma_Ying-jeou's_error-filled_thesis.pdf

[Internal Note] Clive Wilson

[Status changed to *Closed*.]

Dear Ms Wilson:

Thank you very much for your confirmation about President Tsai's PhD degree.

Despite a very strong opposition from her own party, Do. Tsai was nominated as the presidential candidate of the Democratic Progressive Party (DPP) yesterday. We hope she will be re-elected as the President of Taiwan for the next four years despite fake news and false news, naysayers spread by the Chinese in and out of Taiwan.

In fact, the situation is much much more complicated than Premier May in England or the current protest in Hong Kong due to the Chinese and panda huggers' interference.

In any case, "missing" means it existed. That also confirm that she had submitted the PhD thesis, and she graduated. One theory here is that the thesis might be stolen by a Chinese to spread rumor that Tsai concocted her degree to question her integrity.

We are very proud of our President, and her achievements. Please continue looking for her Thesis to help her and let us know.

Incidentally, her Thesis topic was innovative and farsighted in 1984, as the topic of "unfair trade practices" is current very hot under Trump administration. The LSE should be proud of having such a student.

Thank you very much.

PS. I am sending cc to ███████████ and ███████████, the current and the former

## Clive Wilson

Dear ███

in light of recent interest over President Tsai's re-nomination and the possible ambiguity of my previous email, I thought I should add that University of London and LSE records confirm Tsai Ing-wen was correctly awarded a PhD in Law in 1984.
best wishes
Clive

## [Internal Note] Clive Wilson

[Ownership assigned to Clive Wilson]
[Status changed to *Pending*]

## Clive Wilson

Dear ▮

Unfortunately, LSE Library has never had a copy of this thesis.
All PhDs from that period were awarded under the University of London banner and would have been sent first to Senate House Library. As you can appreciate, over the last few years there has been a lot of interest in Dr Tsai's thesis and we have been in correspondence with the University of London about it and extensive searches made. Unfortunately Senate House are unable to find their copy.
I am sorry we cannot help further
yours sincerely
Clive
Clive Wilson
Enquiry Services Manager
LSE Library

## [Internal Note] Sarah Hayward

Hi
Please can you assist with this thesis enquiry?
Please copy us in your reply
Thanks
Sarah
[Status changed to *Pending*.]

## Original Question

PhD thesis search
Dear Sir/Madam:
My name is ▮ I beg your pardon to writing to you.

I am looking for the LSE thesis as follows. I could not find any title in the PhD thesis section in your library. There are only three PhD thesis in 1984 but none of them has the following title.

Could you kindly direct me to access the thesis?
The ethos indicate that it is a "restricted access." May I ask why is it restricted?

Your early response will be greatly appreciated.

---
Title: Unfair trade practices and safeguard actions
Author: Tsai, Ing-Wen
Awarding Body: London School of Economics and Political Science (University of London)
Current Institution:
London School of Economics and Political Science (University of London)
Date of Award: 1984
Availability of Full
Text: Full text unavailable from EThOS. Restricted access.

The biggest degree fraud case in human history

Please contact the current institution's library for further details.

**Attached Files**
- ███████

**Questioner Information**
Name: ███████
Email: ███████

This email is sent from LSE Library in relationship to ticket id #2633151.
Read our privacy policy.

# RE_-A-plea-for-LSE-to-elaborate

**From:** O"Connor,D
**To:** Wilson,Clive
**Subject:** RE: A plea for LSE to elaborate
**Date:** 16 July 2019 11:14:00

Hi Clive,

I think there can be pretty standard reply to this, with some extra information.

Dear ███,

Thank you for your email which has been passed to me.

As has been highlighted in other correspondence, we have checked our records and both the London School of Economics and Political Science and the University of London confirm that Tsai Ing-Wen was correctly awarded a PhD in Law 1984.

President Tsai Ing-wen recently provided the LSE Library with a facsimile copy of the thesis, 'Unfair trade practices and safeguard actions'. This is now available to view in the LSE Library's reading room.

Tsai Ing-wen is the sole author of the thesis listed on the catalogue. The second name —which was of her PhD supervisor - was briefly added to the catalogue in error and has now been removed. We can confirm he was **not** a co-author of the thesis.

Questions regarding a reproduction of the PhD certificate itself should be directed to the University of London.

Kind regards,


**From:** Directorate
**Sent:** 16 July 2019 10:53
**To:** Wilson,Clive <CLIVE.Wilson@lse.ac.uk>
**Cc:** O'Connor,D <D.O'Connor@lse.ac.uk>
**Subject:** FW: A plea for LSE to elaborate

Dear Clive,
I think you are the right person to send the below email to. I am copying Danny O'Connor for information.

Best regards,
Kinga

**From:** ███
**Sent:** 15 July 2019 18:49

**To:** Directorate <Directorate@lse.ac.uk>
**Subject:** A plea for LSE to elaborate

Dear Director Minouche:

Facing the gigantic pressure from the Taiwanese electorate, Dr. Tsai Ing-wen at last had to yield and provided as late as this year a copy of her 1984 PhD. thesis to the LSE Library to keep in records. The record of this replacement copy's co-authorship partially explains my earlier questioning of her English writing competence—wasn't high enough to afford a PhD thesis, judged from an English speech transcript she provided to the Center for Strategic and International Studies in 2016.

With the advent of the attached page,

I hereby write to make a plea for LSE to elaborate on the following issues:

1. Is it allowed or not allowed for two LSE PhD students to co-author a PhD thesis?

2. If the answer is negative, then the rest of the questions can be dropped. If, however, the answer is positive, will each of the two students be awarded a doctorate degree?

3. If the answer is negative, then the rest of the questions can be dropped. If, however, the answer is positive, then why wouldn't Mr. Elliott be called Dr. Elliott all his life before he passed away in 2016 while Ms. Tsai has been enjoying the bright tile of doctor?

4. Does the fact that Mr. Elliott was never called Dr. Elliott imply that he was never awarded a PhD? If Mr. Elliott was never awarded a PhD with the co-authored thesis, why was Ms. Tsai and why was her degree claimed to be "awarded correctly"?

5. On July 10 Dr. Tsai showed to the public her replacement degree certificate which carries not only a "different" wording but also "different" signature, while the Head of the Diploma Production Office states that "Replacement certificates...... will of course still be identical to the original document— same wording, same signature." Does the black-and-white discrepancy imply that Dr. Tsai's replacement certificate might be "fake"?

6. Why would a worldwide famous education institute like TSE allow a PhD thesis to be missing for 35 years without requesting the author to re-submit a copy and have to wait for the Taiwanese electorate uproar over the issue to demand an answer?

7. Why would Dr. Shih Fang-long, the Co-director of TSE's Taiwan Research Program, continue to blame the repeated calls for an answer by the Taiwanese electorate, including many highly esteemed professors, and brazenly refused to provide a once-and-for-all answer to the thesis mystery to end everyone's agony? What is to hide?

8. Would TSE look into the wording and signature discrepancies

described in issue 5 and what would TSE do should the publicly shown PhD certificate prove to be "fake"?

Thank you very much for the patience to read this long email; your answer to any of these eight issues would be highly appreciative to the electorate of the 2020 Taiwanese presidential election. Since Ms. Tsai has been formally nominated a candidate in the election, the Taiwanese electorate's right to know is well justified. Any attempt to lead this issue into a personal privacy should be bluntly rebutted.

Sincerely yours,

███

惡官 3

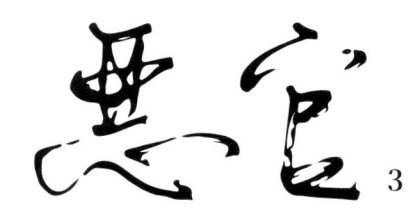

# The Obfuscation of Truth: The Reality and Strategy Within LSE

# The Obfuscation of Truth: The Reality and Strategy Within LSE

The LSE has consistently sidestepped confirming the authenticity of Tsai's credentials. Shih specifically visited LSE to request amendments to the statement from June 24. O'Connor agreed but was displeased with Shih's approach. He found Shih's update pace too slow and her constant directions on the statement's content overbearing.

Dissatisfied with the LSE's statement mentioning Tsai's thesis had dual authors, Shi directly approached O'Connor, demanding he remove this detail. Despite his irritation, O'Connor complied.

Within LSE, there was a confidential notice concerning Tsai's thesis, certificates, and degrees. O'Connor made edits to the language in this notice to circumvent the university's liability. He also crafted a narrative for changing the signature on the certificates to address external queries.

On July 10, 2019, Tsai visited the Taiwanese social media platform Dcard. In front of the media, she displayed her LSE doctoral diploma, reissued in 2015, encased in a plastic bag for about 20 seconds.

Shortly after that, Chu Chun-Chang, the head of the Higher Education Department of Taiwan's Ministry of Education, held a press conference. He stated that, with the assistance of Taiwan's representative office in the UK, they had confirmed the LSE archived Tsai's doctoral thesis.

Yet, on the same day, the Ministry of Education sealed Tsai's employment and promotion records from Soochow University and National Chengchi University in Taiwan as 'document attachments', embargoing them until December 31, 2049.

This series of events further clouded the academic veracity of both LSE and Tsai. The boundary between politics and scholarship were blurred in academia, where truth became intertwined with falsehoods. LSE, an institution of international repute, was facing a question of academic integrity and moral decline.

# RE_-A-plea-for-LSE-to-elaborate

**From:** Wilson, Clive
**To:** ▮
**Subject:** RE: further assistance saught for the whereabouts of a dissertation
**Date:** 12 July 2019 13:25:41

Dear ▮

Ms Orson was using text that I had provided several years ago, and it appears that I had been given incorrect information. It is very unfortunate that Ms Orson's name has been attributed to this text when it was my error. By all means, contact Senate House directly to confirm this.

As to the rest, I'm just a librarian but – as LSE has confirmed the PhD was awarded correctly - I can't see that there are any other questions in your email for LSE to answer.

kind regards


Clive Wilson
Enquiry Services Manager (Academic Services)
London School of Economics      Tel.:   020 7955 7475
10 Portugal Street              Fax.:   020 7955 7454
London WC2A 2HD                 Email:  Datalibrary@lse.ac.uk
                                        clive.wilson@lse.ac.uk


**From:** ▮
**Sent:** 10 July 2019 02:24
**To:** Wilson, Clive
**Cc:** Directorate
**Subject:** further assistance saught for the whereabouts of a dissertation

Dear Manager Wilson:

Thank you very much for the email regarding Dr. Tsai Ing-wen's dissertation. Unfortunately, however, I haven't got the Director's reply as of today, July 9, 2019. Hence my inquiry in the previous email. So, I am particularly appreciative for your email.

No one ever doubts that "Tsai Ing-Wen was correctly awarded a PhD." So, this should not be an issue. However, some controversies have been hovering over Taiwan questioning 1). why should her dissertation be "missing" or "unavailable," (attachment 1) for 35 years, as pointed out by Ms. Ruth Orson, an LSE library assistant at the Research Support Services? Wouldn't every PhD

No one ever doubts that "Tsai Ing-Wen was correctly awarded a PhD." So, this should not be an issue. However, some controversies have been hovering over Taiwan questioning 1). why should her dissertation be "missing" or "unavailable," (attachment 1) for 35 years, as pointed out by Ms. Ruth Orson, an LSE library assistant at the Research Support Services? Wouldn't every PhD holder be proud to show, if not show off, his/her dissertation? If a dissertation author tries best to make the dissertation vanish without a trace, what is there for the author to hide? 2). Why would Dr. Fang-Long Shih, a co-director of Taiwan Research Program, keep trying to translate all questionings regarding this dissertation issue into a political controversy among rivaling candidates in Taiwan's presidential election instead of taking it decently and offering substantial answers since this is really an issue of integrity surrounding a presidential candidate as well as the LSE. Sadly, on June 21, 2019 Dr. Shih again offered the same answer to the same question in the same way as she did four years ago, offering no substantial answers at all except that result would be made available within 10 days, and yet 18 days have passed and the whereabouts of the dissertation is still a mystery. Why so? I can't help but to start to ponder if she is taking a political side, and 3) why would the only page in the record of the dissertation made known so far show no name of the dissertation's supervisor nor the dissertation's abstract (attachment 2)? How would one blame that there are more and more Taiwanese people of all walks who sense something foul in this dissertation mystery.

Shouldn't LSE, being an outstanding university of the oldest democracy, respect Taiwanese people's rights to know about the whereabouts and the contents of the dissertation, particularly when the author is a presidential candidate? Again, this is more an issue of an individual's academic integrity and the LSE's reputation in the world than a political controversy as Dr. Shih tries to lead it to.

Apart from all arguments from all sides, shouldn't LSE and all parties concerned ask Dr Tsai for another copy to keep as record, at least, since none of these parties can find their copies of the dissertation?

Last but not least, I got confused when I was reading your email since you say "It is clear from Senate House Library records that a copy was received." while Ms. Orson of the LSE library informs her inquirer in the said letter, "Unfortunately Senate House apparently never received a copy…" So, I'd appreciate it if you could kindly further clarify this difference of information.

Thank you so much for your kindness to help look into this issue, the result of which is so important for the Taiwanese people to know before they cast their votes in 2020 to choose their new president. The Taiwanese electorate would really appreciate your understanding and caring for their hunger for the rights to know.

Gratefully,

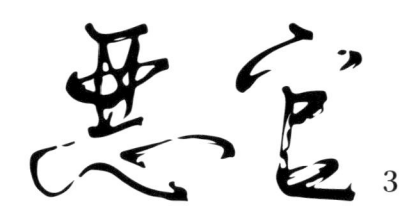

# The Conundrum of Three Certificates: Renewed Doubts Over Tsai's Degree

# The Conundrum of Three Certificates: Renewed Doubts Over Tsai's Degree

Shih penned a letter to the University of London requesting a change in the narrative regarding issuing degree certificates. Concurrently, representatives from the Taiwan Presidential Office met with Donnelly, hoping to obtain Tsai's student records.

A letter from the Taiwan Presidential Office's spokesperson suggested that LSE join in suing scholars and recommended that the institution release a statement based on four points demanded by the Taiwan Presidential Office. LSE's senior management had never anticipated the issue escalating to this extent. Liu Meng-chi, Taiwan's Deputy Minister of Education, decided to visit LSE personally to meet with its Director and other senior officials.

In September 2019, Professor Peng supported Professors Lin and He for a week. Before the Mid-Autumn Festival, the Taiwan Presidential Office issued a late-night press release to sue Professor Peng. Dr. Hsu Yong-tai, a Ph.D. from Oxford University, after examining what was claimed to be Tsai's thesis, published his thoughts in a three-part series in the World Journal, challenging the notion that the black leather-bound volume displayed in LSE 's Women's Library was the formal thesis. Dr. Hsu also wrote to LSE's Law Department requesting an investigation into Tsai's doctoral records, to which the Law Department responded, "No records of Dr. Tsai Ing-wen were preserved."

Under immense public pressure, Tsai finally accepted a media interview to address the doubts about her degree, emphasizing that "if there's a degree, there's a thesis." She dismissed queries with an "It can't be, can it?" The stringent borrowing regulations for the black leather-bound volume at LSE were allegedly imposed by herself.

Meanwhile, the Taiwan Presidential Office held its first press conference on the 'thesis gate,' showcasing page by page of Tsai's thesis drafts with white gloves, though the paper's age appeared inconsistent. On the same day, legislator Kuan Bi-ling from the Democratic Progressive Party disclosed Tsai's third diploma, the one reissued in 2010. The appearance of three diplomas, with two reissued, violated the University of London's rule of allowing only one reissue.

Tsai's last media interaction regarding the thesis controversy occurred during her support trip to Zuoying, Kaohsiung, where she reiterated that the thesis was published into complete books, not just unbound pages, and mentioned that the National Central Library of Taiwan had agreed to archive and make the thesis public. On September 27, 2019, the National Central Library contravened the Degree Conferral Law by including Tsai's supposed thesis on *Unfair Trade Practices and Safeguard Actions* in the Master and Doctoral Thesis Section.

# RE_-A-plea-for-LSE-to-elaborate

**From:** Begum,SS
**To:** Cerny,MW
**Subject:** FW: Ing-wen Tsai"s Ph.D. degree
**Date:** 24 September 2019 08:51:47
**Attachments:** DB5445E9994C44FEA0C59E8128FC71D4.png

Hi Marcus

Forwarding this to you for comment.

Thanks

Shuma

**From:**
**Sent:** 23 September 2019 18:35
**To:** Begum,SS <S.S.Begum@lse.ac.uk>
**Subject:** Ing-wen Tsai's Ph.D. degree

Dear Ms Begum,

I am writing to you to check the authenticity of the Ph.D. degree of Ing-wen Tsai who claims she graduated from LSE in 1984. Tsai's integrity is very important to me and many other people. It is why I send you this email.

People find that Tsai's dissertation is not available in the libraries of LSE or any other public place in the world. It is very suspicious.
Could you check the authenticity of Tsai's Ph.D. degree, please? And what has happened to her dissertation if the Ph.D. degree is authentic?

Followed are some details you may need.

Sincerely,

# RE_-A-plea-for-LSE-to-elaborate

**From:** Wilson,Clive
**To:** Metcalfe,F
**Cc:** O"Connor,D
**Subject:** FW: Request for President Tsai"s student record from Presidential office Taiwan
**Date:** 20 September 2019 11:39:00

Hi Fiona

I'm not sure we would want to do this but this one's also out of my jurisdiction.

Just as far as I can ascertain though: 1 and 2 are definitely correct. 3 and 4 (except for the last point) would come under UoL and not us.

Clive

**From:** ▇▇▇▇▇▇▇▇▇▇▇▇▇▇▇▇
**Sent:** 18 September 2019 10:37
**To:** Wilson,Clive
**Subject:** RE: Request for President Tsai's student record from Presidential office Taiwan

Dear Clive,

As LSE is one of the leading academic institutions in the world, any statement issued by LSE certainly carries weight by itself. We would be truly grateful if you can kindly mention the following points in the statement.

1. University of London and LSE records confirm that Tsai Ing-wen was awarded a PhD in Law in 1984.

2. LSE is in possession of all relevant information pertaining to Dr. Tsai's degree. Dr. Tsai was originally registered as an MPhil student in September 1980. In her second year, upon the recommendation of her supervisor that her work was of doctorate standard, she was retroactively upgraded to PhD status. Dr. Tsai submitted her thesis "Unfair trade practices and safeguard actions", and successfully passed the viva examination in October 1983. She was later awarded a PhD in Law in 1984.

3. This procedure is in line with the School's regulations.

4. A PhD degree is only awarded once a candidate has provided a copy of the successful thesis. While the original copy of Dr. Tsai's thesis cannot currently be located, it is not the only one missing and a hardbound copy of this thesis is currently available at the LSE Library.

As for the channels, is it possible that this statement can be on the LSE website?

Your assistance in clarifying this matter is greatly appreciated.

Sincerely,

▇

**From:** Wilson,Clive [mailto:CLIVE.Wilson@lse.ac.uk]
**Sent:** Tuesday, September 17, 2019 11:53 PM
**To:** ▇
**Subject:** RE: Request for President Tsai's student record from Presidential office Taiwan

Hi ▇

I'm told that LSE isn't really interested in filing a lawsuit. The Comms team seem to be happy to reissue a statement confirming the correct award of the degree but what channel do you think it should go through?

I still haven't seen (or can't find) an English translation of Lin's report.

best wishes

Clive

**From:** ▇
**Sent:** 16 September 2019 13:13
**To:** Wilson,Clive
**Subject:** RE: Request for President Tsai's student record from Presidential office Taiwan

Hi Clive,

I extend my cordial thanks for your help these days.

As you might have noticed, the smear campaign regarding President Tsai's PhD degree has not yet over. On the contrary, the situation deteriorates since LSE has also become one of the targets of the campaign. The campaigners are associating the LSE-Gaddafi affair with this case, ridiculously accusing the school of selling a degree to President Tsai.

Some of the accusations can be found in these two pieces:

Tsai Ing-wen's missing thesis was not submitted says university library
https://richardsonreports.wordpress.com/2019/07/04/tsai-ing-wens-missing-thesis-was-not-submitted-says-university-library/

Tsai Ing-wen files lawsuit against two professors in London School of Economics thesis controversy
https://richardsonreports.wordpress.com/2019/09/06/tsai-ing-wen-files-lawsuit-against-two-professors-in-london-school-of-economics-thesis-controversy/

I would like to recommend the LSE consider issuing statements reconfirming that President Tsai had been awarded a PhD, or filing lawsuit against such smear tactics. Please kindly let me know what's your thought on this matter.

Many thanks,

████

**From:** Wilson,Clive [mailto:CLIVE.Wilson@lse.ac.uk]
**Sent:** Wednesday, September 11, 2019 4:41 PM
**To:** ████
**Subject:** RE: Request for President Tsai's student record from Presidential office Taiwan

H████

as the copy certificate couldn't be obtained from LSE I do doubt that there will be an 'official record' here, but I have passed it on to colleagues who will know more

Clive

**From:** ████
**Sent:** 11 September 2019 07:57
**To:** Wilson,Clive
**Subject:** RE: Request for President Tsai's student record from Presidential office Taiwan

Hi Clive,

Unfortunately, I have not received any response from UoL yet.
Thanks for the information though. I will try to contact ████.
Further, I would like to confirm if LSE holds official records of President Tsai's applications for a degree certification in August 2010 and in September 2015. If LSE does and is able to provide us with the document, we will very much appreciate that.

Best,
████

**From:** Wilson,Clive [mailto:CLIVE.Wilson@lse.ac.uk]
**Sent:** Tuesday, September 10, 2019 10:46 PM
**To:** ████
**Subject:** RE: Request for President Tsai's student record from Presidential office Taiwan

Hi ████

Have you had a reply yet? The only other person I can think of is ███████████
████████████████████████████████████████ and did most of the
investigation work at their end when President Tsai first stood for office. I don't know if she is
still there.

best wishes

Clive

**From:** ███████████████████████
**Sent:** 06 September 2019 06:32
**To:** Wilson,Clive
**Subject:** RE: Request for President Tsai's student record from Presidential office Taiwan

Hi Clive,

Thank you very much for the suggestion. Unfortunately, the contact person at UoL has not replied my email yet.
However, the official records from the school(either LSE or UoL) of President Tsai's applications for a degree certification in August 2010 and in September 2015 are necessary to rebut the accusation, which claims that the certificate we provided was not issued by the school and therefore, was fake.

Do you have suggestion that from which sector I can possibly get this information?

Many thanks,
███

**From:** Wilson,Clive [mailto:CLIVE.Wilson@lse.ac.uk]
**Sent:** Tuesday, September 3, 2019 11:06 PM
**To:** ███████████████
**Subject:** RE: Request for President Tsai's student record from Presidential office Taiwan

Hi ███

You might have done this already but it occurs to me that you should also contact the University of London directly. Due to the umbrella nature of the UoL, especially pre 2010, their student record will be different to ours.

best wishes

Clive

**From:** ███████████████████████

**Sent:** 03 September 2019 06:53
**To:** Wilson,Clive
**Cc:** Donnelly,S
**Subject:** RE: Request for President Tsai's student record from Presidential office Taiwan

Dear Mr. Clive Wilson and Ms. Sue Donnelly,

Attached is the scanned letter signed by President Tsai.

We expect the academic record to contain information such as date of her viva exam, date of notification of the exam results, date of degree awarded, date of her application for a degree certification(If memory serves, it should be in August 2010 and in September 2015).

Please feel free to let me know if there is anything I can help and million thanks for your assistance.

Sincerely,

---

**From:** Wilson,Clive [mailto:CLIVE.Wilson@lse.ac.uk]
**Sent:** Monday, September 2, 2019 6:31 PM
**To:**
**Cc:** Donnelly,S <S.Donnelly@lse.ac.uk>
**Subject:** RE: Request for President Tsai's student record from Presidential office Taiwan

Dear

yes, we heard about the report last week and look forward to seeing an English version.

We can definitely provide a copy of President Tsai's student record but we do need to have a letter actually signed by President Tsai to do this. This can be a scan and it can request that the record is sent to you but as it is her personal data, the letter has to be signed by her.

I have copied this to Ms. Sue Donnelly, the LSE Archivist, so if you can send the scanned letter to both of us we can sort that out for you.

best wishes

Clive

---

**From:**
**Sent:** 02 September 2019 11:02
**To:** Wilson,Clive
**Subject:** Request for President Tsai's student record from Presidential office Taiwan

120  The biggest degree fraud case in human history

Dear Clive,

I trust this e-mail finds you well. It's been a while since our last conversation. Is everything going well with you?

I am writing to again seek your kind assistance with regard to President Tsai's LSE doctoral degree. To rebut the defamatory libel, President Tsai decides to take legal actions against the people behind the malice. For the court proceeding, President Tsai will need her student record, including the beginning and ending dates of study, names of supervisor and viva examiners… etc.

In our email trail, you kindly notified us that LSE has identified related documentation in this regard. I am wondering if it is possible that the above-mentioned information can be retrieved and sent to us? We have applied for the certificate of the degree for her, but more detail would be necessary to clarify the speculation.

There is another thing that I would like you to know. Recently, there is a publication by ▓▓▓▓▓▓ titled, "An independent investigation: the authenticity of Tsai, Ing Wen's doctoral degree and thesis." In the report, he states that LSE, as an accomplice, has helped Dr. Tsai to fake her degree. The English version is expected to be released by ▓ this week. You may look into it and decide whether it is necessary for the school to issue a statement against the unreasonable accusation as LSE is one of the leading academic institutions in the world and any statement issued by LSE certainly carries weight by itself.

We appreciate your help on this matter.


Sincerely yours,
▓▓▓▓▓
Spokesperson of the President
Office of the President, ROC(Taiwan)

The biggest degree fraud case in human history

惡官 3

**The Enigma of the Black Leather-Bound Thesis: Taiwan's Representatives Visit LSE**

# The Enigma of the Black Leather-Bound Thesis: Taiwan's Representatives Visit LSE

In July 2019, the narrative surrounding the entire incident took a sudden turn. It became the prevailing statement that Tsai's thesis had once been submitted to the University of London's main library.

The Taiwanese Representative Office in the UK decided to take matters into its own hands and visit LSE in pursuit of the truth. Shortly after that, Taiwan's Ministry of Education dispatched its representatives and held a press conference in Taiwan, attempting to clarify the unfolding events.

But the truth seemed to become increasingly elusive. The so-called "black leather-bound" thesis submitted by Tsai to LSE, believed to be vital to unveiling the truth, appeared to be concealed from the public eye.

The lines between truth and falsehood, power and ethics, politics and scholarship were becoming increasingly blurred in the academic realm. Wilson, the University of London, LSE itself, and Tsai have all emerged as key players in this controversy, while the truth still awaits revelation.

# FW_ Taiwan Deputy Minister visiting LSE

| From: | Directorate |
|---|---|
| To: | Ross,LV |
| Cc: | Directorate |
| Subject: | FW: Taiwan Deputy Minister visiting LSE |
| Date: | 18 September 2019 10:17:54 |

From ███████████ Ministry of Foreign Affairs – Taiwan. Wanting to speak to Minouche on short notice.

Fri 20 Sept won't work but if Minouche was keen, it looks like Monday 23 Sept might work at 3-5pm?

Best,
Daniel


**From:** ███████████████████
**Sent:** 18 September 2019 10:13
**To:** Directorate <Directorate@lse.ac.uk>
**Subject:** Taiwan Deputy Minister visiting LSE

Dear Dame Minouche,

My office, the Education Division of the Taipei Representative Office in the UK, is the official representation of the Ministry of Education, Taiwan (MoE), and a department of the *de facto* embassy for Taiwan. Our responsibilities include striving to enhance educational relations between the UK and Taiwan, promoting the study of Mandarin at institutions in the UK and facilitating study abroad.

The Deputy Minister for Education in Taiwan, Mr Mon-Chi Lio, will be arriving in London later this week to attend the UK-Taiwan Higher Education Forum. The Forum will be attended by the Presidents of seventeen Taiwanese national universities as well as representatives, including Vice-Chancellors, from around thirty UK universities.

As no representatives from LSE will be joining the Forum, Mr Lio would very much like to pay a courtesy call to your office in order to thank you in person for displaying a copy of President Tsai's thesis in the LSE Library.

Mr Lio has a tight schedule, but could be available on the 20th September from 3:30pm - 6pm or on the 23rd September from 10:30am -12pm / 3pm-5pm.

We appreciate this is very short notice and you must be extremely busy, but would that time potentially be convenient for you for a brief meeting with the Deputy Minister?

I look forward to hearing from you.

Kind regards,

███████████████

# RE_ an odd request for truth

**From:** O"Connor,D
**To:** Thomson,MT
**Subject:** RE: an odd request for truth
**Date:** 26 September 2019 14:17:35

Thanks Mark,

This is getting quite frustrating.

Danny

**From:** Thomson,MT
**Sent:** 26 September 2019 12:23
**To:** O'Connor,D <D.O'Connor@lse.ac.uk>
**Subject:** FW: an odd request for truth

Of possible interest.

**From:** ▇▇▇▇▇▇▇▇▇▇▇▇▇▇▇▇
**Sent:** 26 September 2019 12:21
**To:** Thomson,MT <M.T.Thomson@lse.ac.uk>
**Subject:** Re: an odd request for truth

Dear Mr. Thomson,

It is truly kind of you to reply this email.

If so, according to Ms. Tsai, LSE did lose her thesis and therefore should take the blame. I just couldn't imagine how this could happen to all three libraries in the University of London, that is, the Senate Library, IALS Library and LSE library. There must be black holes or stargates in those libraries. By the way, in a press conference that was held two days ago, Ms. Tsai admitted that the facsimile copy was merely a manuscript and not a completed thesis.

Thank you so much for your time.

Sincerely yours,

▇▇▇▇▇

Thomson,MT <M.T.Thomson@lse.ac.uk> 於 2019年9月26日 週四 上午3:12寫道:

> Dear ▇▇▇▇▇,
>
> The London School of Economics and Political Science and the University of London can categorically confirm that Dr Tsai Ing-Wen completed her thesis and was correctly awarded a PhD in Law in 1984.
>
> Dr Tsai Ing-wen recently provided the LSE Library with a facsimile copy of the thesis, 'Unfair trade practices and safeguard actions'. This is available to view in the LSE library reading room upon request.
>
> All best,

Mark Thomson
Academic Registrar

**From:** ██████████████████████████
**Sent:** 25 September 2019 03:32
**To:** Thomson,MT <M.T.Thomson@lse.ac.uk>
**Subject:** an odd request for truth

Dear Mr. Thomson

This is ████████████████████████████████████████████
████████████████████████████████████████████████████
████████████ Nonetheless, I do not write this email for my personal matter, but for truth.

Recently, a Taiwanese LSE graduate tried hard to prove that she did get a Ph.D. degree in Law in your school in 1984. And yet, the more evidence she provided, the more curious the truth became. This graduate happens to be the president of Taiwan, Ing-wen Tsai. She provided her LSE student record and notification of examination outcome (please see the attached files), but they just arouse more questions. For example, the notification is lacking a signature of the academic registrar, that is, Mrs. G. F. Roberts, which is very strange. Or, why the registrar crossed out "MPhil" and replace it with "Ph.D." in handwriting without any notes (maybe it was different in 1980). There are still more questions like these.

Many young and high intellectuals in Taiwan like me are playing Sherlock Holmes now -- that is why I send this odd email to you. I don't expect to get all the answers. If you couldn't confirm if those documents came from your office, would you please at least give me a hint about one question -- how would your office put a Taiwanese student's nationality in the student record in the past (1980) and in the present -- Republic of China (ROC) or Taiwan?

Thank you very much for reading this email. Wish you all the best.

P.S.: The first attachment is President Tsai's student record provided by her spokesman, which she said came from LSE. The second attachment is a comparative analysis of the notification of exam outcome by another Holmes on the internet (he found another Ph.D. graduate's letter on the internet) and found many strange things.

Sincerely yours
████

恶官 3

# LSE's Strategy:
# Canned Responses and Image Management

# LSE's Strategy:
# Canned Responses and Image Management

At the University of Tokyo's law library, a student browsing through ancient texts stumbled upon a document dubbed the "Red Book." The existence of this book was undeniably a huge surprise for LSE. The upper echelons within their institution privately rejoiced, "This is great, if the book is genuine, then all our previous concerns will be dissipated."

However, the University of Tokyo student further revealed that he had found a 1985 publication in the library's catalog, which listed Tsai's doctoral thesis. This seemed to corroborate that Tsai indeed received her Ph.D. in 1984. Yet, Professor Peng, a web show host, questioned this, pointing out that finding a catalog entry is not tantamount to finding the book itself. He noted that in his search of the records at the Institute of Advanced Legal Studies in the UK, Tsai's library record was notably absent.

On his show "True Voice of Taiwan," Peng further questioned the disparity, saying that a book is not the same as a catalog entry; having a book doesn't always mean there's an entry, and an entry doesn't guarantee the existence of the book. He asserted that the controversy over Tsai's thesis must be confronted directly on "the main road of proper procedure," stressing that the thesis hasn't appeared in 36 years, not as a manuscript, a book, or even a catalog entry.

The University of Tokyo student retorted that unless Tsai had the immense power to forge a 1985 publication and remembered to archive a copy even across the sea at the University of Tokyo's library, there seems to be no doubt about her having obtained a Ph.D.

Peng reiterated his skepticism about the publication, stating that its foreword clearly indicates that the book does not record actual degree conferrals. Chinese scholar Li Haimo also analyzed online that the IALS index is a dynamic record of all legal research topics by master's and doctoral candidates, and indeed many listed did not go on to obtain a Ph.D.

Nevertheless, this academic tempest was far from over. Facing external scrutiny, LSE decided on a strategy: to issue prepared "canned responses" to inquiries they deemed unfriendly. Such a tactic is undoubtedly aimed at preserving the institution's image but has also sparked considerable controversy.

Taiwanese officials, under intense media scrutiny during a Presidential Office press conference, felt the pressure mounting. They requested another meeting with LSE, hoping to glean more information. The Taiwan Presidential Office specifically asked LSE to provide details about the doctoral study process from the 1980s, in hopes of clarifying the true nature of the event.

At the heart of this storm, O'Connor is a pivotal figure. Even while on vacation, he would occasionally send group emails, "reminding" everyone to be mindful of certain matters.

With the arrival of Liu, LSE began to prepare for the reception. They were aware that this meeting would be critical in determining the direction of the entire incident. Internally, emotions at LSE were complex. In response to external questions, they opted for a strategy: issuing preformulated "canned responses" to queries they perceived as unfriendly. This approach, undoubtedly meant to protect the school's reputation, nevertheless engendered even more controversy.

# RE_ Evidence of Tsai's Ph.D. submission (1)

| | |
|---|---|
| **From:** | Wilson,Clive |
| **To:** | O"Connor,D; Phdacademy |
| **Cc:** | Metcalfe,F; Thomson,MT |
| **Subject:** | RE: Evidence of Tsai PhD submission |
| **Date:** | 27 September 2019 13:57:24 |

I've found our copy of the book the student found and made a quick video (because I am sad!):
https://photos.app.goo.gl/w9GwFXGq2hYn8atFA

This book is in a number of UK libraries and several in Germany, Holland and Spain. It was reviewed in at least two law journals.

And yes, a copy of the thesis with no missing pages would be nice ☺

The National Central Library has now made the digitised version available through https://etds.ncl.edu.tw/cgi-bin/gs32/gsweb.cgi/ccd=9aF5rF/webmge?switchlang=en It is a beautifully clean copy, with none of the scruffy photocopying of our copy ...

And I think they are still hoping LSE will make a repeat statement ... although if they do supply us with an online copy, could we do it then?

thanks

Clive

**From:** O'Connor,D
**Sent:** 27 September 2019 10:01
**To:** Wilson,Clive; Phdacademy
**Cc:** Metcalfe,F; Thomson,MT
**Subject:** RE: Evidence of Tsai PhD submission

Thanks Clive.

Probably worth going and taking a photo of the hard copy of the IALS index when you can. This isn't going away!

(I assume you mean to new copy will *include* the missing pages?)

Danny

**From:** Wilson,Clive
**Sent:** 27 September 2019 09:54
**To:** Phdacademy <Phdacademy@lse.ac.uk>; O'Connor,D <D.O'Connor@lse.ac.uk>
**Cc:** Metcalfe,F <F.Metcalfe@lse.ac.uk>; Thomson,MT <M.T.Thomson@lse.ac.uk>
**Subject:** RE: Evidence of Tsai PhD submission

Ha, that's fantastic.
I was actually planning a visit to IALS to look at the old printed version of Index to Theses for

exactly the same reason (we didn't keep it once it went electronic).

I'm batting away about one enquiry a day at the moment.

You may also have seen that the President's office announced on Monday that she would put an electronic copy in Taiwan's theses depository. They have also offered us a copy (and a replacement printed copy that doesn't have the missing pages!)

Clive

**From:** LSE PhD Academy [mailto:phdacademy@lse.ac.uk]
**Sent:** 27 September 2019 09:44
**To:** O'Connor,D
**Cc:** Metcalfe,F; Wilson,Clive; Thomson,MT
**Subject:** RE: Evidence of Tsai PhD submission

Thanks Danny,

Sporadic queries continue to trickle in as very badly disguised 'official' requests for verification. I'm not sure how authoritative people think a generic yahoo account and a one line signature with a made up job title and organisation looks.

Regards,
Marcus

**Marcus Cerny**
**PhD Academy Deputy Director**
The London School of Economics and Political Science
Houghton Street, London WC2A 2AE
t: +44 (0)20 7955 6766
e: m.w.cerny@lse.ac.uk
lse.ac.uk/phdacademy

If you are a current PhD student please remember to send your queries through the PhD Academy Enquiry Form. All other enquirers should contact phdacademy@lse.ac.uk

--------------- Original Message ---------------
**From:** O'Connor,D [d.o'connor@lse.ac.uk]
**Sent:** 26/09/2019 16:51
**To:** clive.wilson@lse.ac.uk; m.t.thomson@lse.ac.uk; phdacademy@lse.ac.uk
**Cc:** f.metcalfe@lse.ac.uk
**Subject:** Evidence of Tsai PhD submission

Dear all,

I thought you may be interested to see the recent report in the pro-Tsai Taiwan News.
https://www.taiwannews.com.tw/en/news/3784704

It seems someone uncovered a IALS listings document which included an entry for her thesis.

Thanks,

Danny

**From:** Windebank,S
**Sent:** 26 September 2019 16:38
**To:** O'Connor,D <D.O'Connor@lse.ac.uk>
**Subject:** FW: Google Alert - "London School of Economics"

Interesting (it's good news, if true)

**From:** Google Alerts [mailto:googlealerts-noreply@google.com]
**Sent:** 26 September 2019 05:57
**To:** Windebank,S <S.Windebank@lse.ac.uk>
**Subject:** Google Alert - "London School of Economics"

## "London School of Economics"

As-it-happens update · 26 September 2019

NEWS

### 1985 Todai library document lists Taiwan president's LSE Ph.D. dissertation
Taiwan News
... published in 1985 that clearly lists Taiwan President Tsai Ing-wen's (???) Ph.D. from **London School of Economics** and Political Science (LSE).

You have received this email because you have subscribed to **Google Alerts**.
Unsubscribe

Receive this alert as RSS feed

Send Feedback

ref:_00D58JYzR._5004ItwAJi:ref

132  The biggest degree fraud case in human history

# RE_ Ing Wen Tsai's thesis gate

**From:** Directorate
**To:** O"Connor,D
**Subject:** RE: Ing Wen Tsai"s thesis gate
**Date:** 30 September 2019 17:02:00

Thank you very much for your advice!
Best regards,
Kinga

**From:** O'Connor,D
**Sent:** 30 September 2019 17:00
**To:** Directorate <Directorate@lse.ac.uk>; Wilson,Clive <CLIVE.Wilson@lse.ac.uk>
**Subject:** RE: Ing Wen Tsai's thesis gate

It may be best if you pass them to Communications so we can reply.

(Though I understand ▇▇▇ has already had a number of replies, so we've exhausted that route).

Kind regards,

Danny


**From:** Directorate
**Sent:** 30 September 2019 16:57
**To:** O'Connor,D <D.O'Connor@lse.ac.uk>; Wilson,Clive <CLIVE.Wilson@lse.ac.uk>
**Subject:** RE: Ing Wen Tsai's thesis gate

How shall I reply to these in the future? Do you have some kind of a template? Or suggestion on how I should reply?

Best regards,
Kinga

**From:** O'Connor,D
**Sent:** 30 September 2019 13:59
**To:** Directorate <Directorate@lse.ac.uk>; Wilson,Clive <CLIVE.Wilson@lse.ac.uk>
**Subject:** RE: Ing Wen Tsai's thesis gate

Thanks Kinga.

These individuals are not well-intentioned actors so I think we should still provide only basic information.

Danny

**From:** Directorate
**Sent:** 30 September 2019 13:32
**To:** Wilson,Clive <CLIVE.Wilson@lse.ac.uk>; O'Conror,D <D.O'Connor@lse.ac.uk>
**Subject:** FW: Ing Wen Tsai's thesis gate

Dear Clive and Daniel,
I keep ignoring this individual as you have mentioned in one of your last emails, but just to let you know he or she is still sending us emails from time to time.

Best regards,
Kinga

**From:** ▓▓▓▓▓▓▓▓▓▓▓▓▓▓▓▓▓▓▓▓▓▓
**Sent:** 29 September 2019 13:15
**To:** Directorate <Directorate@lse.ac.uk>
**Subject:** Ing Wen Tsai's thesis gate

Dear Director Minouche:

Now that Ing-wen Tsai has publicly denied in a Taipei press conference her knowledge of all the LSE banning restrictions imposed on her Ph.D. thesis, I am eager to know if all the restrictions to the access to her thesis will be lifted immediately. In the public denial, which has been repeatedly played in Taiwan's TV news and comment programs, Tsai clearly stated that she was not aware of any of such banning restrictions. What people can't understand after Tsai's denial is why LSE would state in the first place in the displayed thesis to restrict copying of any part of this thesis". Also, since Tsai's president office has made the thesis available in Taiwan's Central Library, LSE's continuous restrictions on her thesis displayed on campus seems to have become a joke.

Also, I'd appreciate it if you, an honorable and highly respected LSE Director, could lead an investigation to see why Tsai could be awarded a doctorate degree when LSE library, the Senate House Library and the IALS repeatedly stated that none of them have ever received a copy or unable to find their copy of Tsai's thesis, while Article 58 of the LSE Regulations for Research Degrees clearly states that a Ph.D. degree "will not be awarded until the candidate has provided a copy of the successful thesis". Intriguingly, the non-existence of Tsai's thesis remains until Aug 26, 2019, when a photo copy from her personal collection was finally made available by LSE.

As more and more renowned Ph.D. holding scholars getting involved in the proactive investigations of Tsai Ing-wen's "Thesis Gate" and digging out more proof and questioning points, their suspicions over the authenticity of Tsai's thesis has become more and more persuasive and justifiable. An LSE Director over 35 years away, you have everyone's confidence that you are not part of this "potential scandal." As a result, you make an ideal objective third-party to lead an objective investigation into this highly controversial gate. Given the fact that Tsai being one of the three already known candidates in Taiwan's presidential election in January 2020, the importance of this investigation is self-evident. Countless Taiwanese electorates have claimed that a candidate that can't even explained why her thesis should have been missing on records for over 35 years and can't provide a degree certificate carrying a formal embossing LSE seal should be excluded from the candidate list until all the questionable issues have been clarified.

Other questionings raised by American and British Ph.D. holding scholars and the Taiwanese journalists which Tsai Ing-wen has never answered include but are not limited to the followings:

> 1. why a highly respected university like LSE would accept and display a thesis that has so many defects such as missing 6 pages, carrying so many nonconsecutive pages and most importantly, discussing only the first half of its topic, the unfair trade practices, leaving a total blank on the second part of the thesis, and safeguard actions—not a single sentence/word was contributed to the safeguard actions, let alone a conclusion of the whole thesis.
>
> 2. Why would LSE lose Tsai's thesis? Tsai's president office has publicly blamed LSE for losing her thesis and claimed the student who turned in her thesis is not and/or should not be responsible for the loss.
>
> 3. In Tsai's publicized thesis, she keeps using the plural first person "we," matching first LSE record of Tsai's thesis showing two author's names. Why would LSE later claim it was a mistake and changed it into a one-authored thesis?
>
> 4. Tsai showed on TV programs her self-claimed "original" copy of her Ph.D. degree certificate. Then why would she have to apply twice for replacement copies of her degree copies?

My personal question is as follows: Is this somehow related to a website that sells a Ph.D. thesis under the topic of "Unfair Trade Exercises" for current price of $13.90 a page? Please note that the topic sold carries only "Unfair Trade Practices"—exactly the same wording as the first half of Tsai's thesis topic and doesn't touch the "safe guard" part at all, exactly the same as how Tsai Ing-wen dealt with her thesis.

Thank you very much for your time and patience to read through this message. Your kind investigation into this highly controversial gate would be really appreciated by all Taiwanese electorates.

Sincerely,

# RE_ Inquire From Taipei Representative Office

**From:** Wilson,Clive
**To:** Cerny,MW
**Subject:** RE: Inquire From Taipei Representative Office--Education Division
**Date:** 04 September 2019 10:06:25

Hi Marcus

no problem -- I knew the second part was definitely them but, thought I'd better start with you. ☺

thanks for the confirmation.

Clive

**From:** Cerny,MW
**Sent:** 04 September 2019 10:04
**To:** Wilson,Clive
**Subject:** RE: Inquire From Taipei Representative Office--Education Division

Hi Clive,

I think that is something for the UofL to clarify. My knowledge would go back to the late 1990's and that is not robust.

The physical thesis submission for examination will have been handled by the Research Degrees Office at UofL and the final copy by Senate House Library.

Sorry about this rather unhelpful response. I am confident in my assumption as to what will have been the process even at that time (confirmation that the thesis had been passed by the examiners, hard bound copy to Senate House triggering confirmation of award by RDO and placing in the Library) but this should be clarified by UofL and I would direct President Tsai's office to send queries on this process to them.

Thanks,
Marcus

**Marcus Cerny**
Deputy Director, PhD Academy
London School of Economics and Political Science
Houghton Street
London WC2A 2AE

Please consider the environment and do not print this email unless absolutely necessary.
Please access the attached hyperlink for an important electronic communications disclaimer: http://lse.ac.uk/emailDisclaimer

**From:** Wilson,Clive
**Sent:** 04 September 2019 09:45
**To:** Cerny,MW
**Subject:** FW: Inquire From Taipei Representative Office--Education Division

Hi Marcus

Are you able to answer this? Or at least the first part... UoL processes obviously for them to answer.

As a quick update, I don't know if you are aware but a North American-Taiwan professor came in over the summer to look at Ingwen Tsai's thesis. He published a 50 page report (in Chinese) last week, criticising it and alluding to Gaddafi again. President Tsai has decided to take him to court, hence the questions. She has also requested and been sent a copy of her student record.

thanks

Clive

**From:** ▮▮▮▮▮▮▮▮▮▮▮▮▮▮
**Sent:** 04 September 2019 09:39
**To:** Wilson,Clive
**Cc:** sztseng
**Subject:** RE: Inquire From Taipei Representative Office--Education Division

Dear Clive,

The biggest degree fraud case in human history    137

Thank you so much for your response.

The President's Office has asked me to find out what the procedure was back in the 1980s for PhD students to submit their theses. Do you know what they would be required to do and how the University of London would process and catalogue the theses submitted at that time?

If you are not in a position to answer this question, would you be able to suggest a contact person who might be able to help explain the process?

Kind regards,

████

████

Taipei Representative Office in the U.K.
Tel: +44+20 7436 5888
-----Original message-----
From: Wilson, Clive <CLIVE.Wilson@lse.ac.uk>
To: ████
Cc: ████, O'Connor,D <D.O'Connor@lse.ac.uk>
Date: Fri, 30 Aug 2019 10:37:12
Subject: RE: Inquire From Taipei Representative Office--Education Division

Hi ████

thanks for the email. All's well here. It had gone quiet briefly and I was made aware that ████ had visited whilst I was on
leave. I did wonder what would happen next.

To answer the questions:

All visitors to LSE must complete the application form at:
https://www.lse.ac.uk/library/using-the-library/secure/join-the-library

and specify which material they wish to view. All applications to view printed theses in our collections will be accepted and an appointment made to view them in our Special Collections Reading Room.

The copy we hold was received on the 10th July 2019.

We do not know if other theses were missing from the transfer list but received over 600 theses that had not originally been presented to LSE at the time of their award.

As we have just seen the news that says President Tsai may take legal action, I am copying my reply to Danny O'Connor our Head of Media Relations

very best wishes

Clive

Clive Wilson

Enquiry Services Manager (Academic Services)

London School of Economics Tel.: 020 7955 7475

10 Portugal Street Fax.: 020 7955 7454

London WC2A 2HD Email:
Datalibrary@lse.ac.uk

clive.wilson@lse.ac.uk

From:
█████████████████████

Sent: 29 August 2019 14:14
To: Wilson,Clive

Cc: ███████████████
Subject: Inquire From Taipei Representative Office--Education Division

Dear Clive,

I hope you have been keeping well and enjoying the hot weather.

It was very kind of you to welcome my colleagues and me to the LSE Library in mid-July and to allow us to view and photograph President Tsai's thesis. You may be aware that another press conference was held in Taiwan today regarding President Tsai's PhD degree. During this press conference, a Professor by the name of ███████ concluded that President Tsai's PhD was not valid, raising various questions which we are now obliged to address.

Therefore, could I possibly trouble you to answer the following three questions?

1. What is the procedure for a visitor to apply to view President Tsai's thesis in the LSE Library?

2. When did the LSE Library receive the copy of President Tsai's thesis that it currently holds?

3. Was President Tsai's thesis the only one not to be included in the transfer list from the University of London to LSE Library or was this the case with other theses, as well?

If you would prefer to respond to these questions in person, would it be possible for me to arrange another meeting with you at the LSE Library at some point tomorrow (Friday 30th Aug.)? Otherwise, I look forward to receiving your reply by e-mail.

Thank you very much indeed for your continued assistance in this case.

Kind regards,

惡官 3

## The Enigma of the Women's Library: The Mystery of Tsai's Thesis Storage

# The Enigma of the Women's Library: The Mystery of Tsai's Thesis Storage

Professor Peng initiated the demand for proof of Tsai's thesis, but LSE decided to remain silent, refusing external responses. This deepened concerns about LSE, particularly regarding uncertainties surrounding Tsai's student records.

Tensions rose within LSE. They felt uneasy about their responses, especially when the external inquiries delved into the details of Tsai's oral examination. Despite LSE's emphatic stance that Tsai had obtained the degree, it seemed insufficient to quell external skepticism.

In this context, Haynes became a focal point. Initially earnest in his new role, he quickly got entangled in the controversy. O'Connor admitted to him that Tsai's published thesis wasn't the final version. Cerny cautioned him against saying too much. Wilson asserted that the restrictions on Tsai's thesis were no different from others.

However, the controversy did not subside. O'Connor strongly urged LSE not to engage with Professor Lin, believing his actions heightened internal tensions. LSE initiated internal meetings to discuss crisis management.

O'Connor asserted that Tsai's thesis wasn't stored only in the Women's Library. Still, LSE's explanation for why it was placed there remained vague. Unhappy with being labeled a deceiver by the public, O'Connor considered the school's scrutiny as political misinformation. In October 2019, the controversy reached its peak. LSE published a statement on its official website attempting to put an end to the turmoil. Tsai also posted on Facebook, urging people to share the conclusion to the controversy.

However, the turmoil persisted. During legislative questioning, Legislator Chen asked how many of the 48 national university presidents believed in the authenticity of Tsai's degree. Only six raised their hands, escalating the controversy once again.

Professor Peng led a delegation to London for an on-site investigation. They interviewed librarians at LSE and proved that the school had never archived this thesis.

Richardson filed a request with LSE under the Freedom of Information Act, seeking disclosure of Tsai's oral examination committee and date. However, LSE's response sparked even more significant controversy.

# Fwd_ Request for information

**From:** Winterstein,J
**To:** O"Connor,D
**Subject:** Fwd: Request for information
**Date:** 03 October 2019 08:51:17

Hi Danny

The story that will not die! If you'd like me to get back to him could you send me our latest statement to pass on?

Many thanks
Jess

Begin forwarded message:

**From:** ▮
**Date:** 2 October 2019 at 23:56:14 BST
**To:** j.winterstein@lse.ac.uk
**Subject: Request for information**

I am working on an article about the controversy surrounding Republic of China in-exile President Tsai Ing-wen's LSE graduate thesis. Ms. Tsai filed her 1984 theis with the LSE Library in 2019 and that has generated much public interest in Taiwan. The name of the thesis is "Unfair Trade Practices and Safeguard Actions."

My questions, for publication, are:

1) What is the name and degree of Tsai Ing-wen's LSE Advisor?
2) What are the names of the thesis Examiners?
3) What is the date of the thesis oral review?
4) What is the date of the Examiner's signatures of approval?

If you are not the correct person to handle this information request please forward to the appropriate individual.

Thank you for your attention to this request.

# RE_ for truth and truth only，ligitimately

**From:** O"Connor,D
**To:** Haynes,KJ; Cerny,MW
**Cc:** Metcalfe,F; Thomson,MT
**Subject:** RE: for truth and truth only, ligitimately
**Date:** 01 October 2019 16:06:57

On reflection, it seems weird that you've answered one question but ignored all the others.

I've updated a standard reply we've been using below:

Dear xxx

As indicated to a number of enquirers, the London School of Economics and Political Science and the University of London can confirm categorically that Tsai Ing-Wen completed and submitted her thesis and was correctly awarded a PhD in Law in 1984.

[Update] For your information, Dr Tsai Ing-wen recently provided the LSE Library with a facsimile copy of the thesis, *Unfair trade practices and safeguard actions*. I understand a digital copy has also been provided to Taiwan's National Central Library.
https://ndltd.ncl.edu.tw/cgi-bin/gs32/gsweb.cgi/ccd=1wi2HF/webmge?mode=basic

regards,

**From:** Haynes,KJ
**Sent:** 01 October 2019 15:58
**To:** O'Connor,D <D.O'Connor@lse.ac.uk>; Cerny,MW <M.W.Cerny@lse.ac.uk>
**Cc:** Metcalfe,F <F.Metcalfe@lse.ac.uk>; Thomson,MT <M.T.Thomson@lse.ac.u<>
**Subject:** RE: for truth and truth only, ligitimately

Thanks, Danny. Are you comfortable with the following response?

Dear ▮▮▮▮▮

Thank you for your email of 1 October 2019.

We can confirm that President Tsai successfully completed a PhD at LSE in 1984. As was normal practice for LSE qualifications in 1984, her academic certificate was issued by the University of London, of which our School has been a member institution since the beginning of the 20th Century.

As do most institutions in the United Kingdom, the University of London has in place a procedure where it is able to re-issue certificates on request. This practice may explain the existence of more recently issued academic certificates to which you refer.

Best wishes, Kevin

LSE Legal Team
Secretary's Division
Room 3.01, 1 Kingsway
London School of Economics and Political Science
Houghton Street
London
WC2A 2AE

020 7955 7823

**From:** O'Connor,D
**Sent:** 01 October 2019 15:11
**To:** Haynes,KJ <K.J.Haynes@lse.ac.uk>; Cerny,MW <M.W.Cerny@lse.ac.uk>
**Cc:** Metcalfe,F <F.Metcalfe@lse.ac.uk>; Thomson,MT <M.T.Thomson@lse.ac.uk>
**Subject:** RE: for truth and truth only, ligitimately

Hi Kevin,

In general we have been giving a two line reply effectively saying, her PhD is legitimate. The main reason for this nonsense is that the UoL / IALS lost her thesis, probably many years ago.

On the certificates – these were issued by the University of London. Any graduate can ask for certificates to be re-issued if they pay a small fee. I understand from UoL that she did, indeed, ask for two additional copies.

On everything else, I don't have relevant information on signatures and dates, I'm not totally sure it's worth responding to each question as it's just going to invite never-ending questions.

Danny


**From:** Haynes,KJ
**Sent:** 01 October 2019 15:05
**To:** O'Connor,D <D.O'Connor@lse.ac.uk>; Cerny,MW <M.W.Cerny@lse.ac.uk>
**Cc:** Metcalfe,F <F.Metcalfe@lse.ac.uk>; Thomson,MT <M.T.Thomson@lse.ac.uk>
**Subject:** FW: for truth and truth only, ligitimately

Hello Danny, Marcus

You'll see below that I've been approached by a member of ▇▇▇▇▇▇ staff looking for clarity on President Tsai's qualifications from LSE (or the University of London).

I'm happy to respond, or for anyone else to do so. Could you please confirm the facts (when, where, what) of the situation if you're content for me to respond?

Best wishes, Kevin

LSE Legal Team
Secretary's Division
Room 3 01, 1 Kingsway
London School of Economics and Political Science
Houghton Street
London
WC2A 2AE

020 7955 7823

**From:** ▇▇▇▇▇▇▇▇▇▇▇▇▇▇▇▇▇▇▇▇
**Sent:** 01 October 2019 02:47
**To:** Haynes,KJ <K.J.Haynes@lse.ac.uk>
**Subject:** for truth and truth only, ligitimately

Dear Mr. Haynes,

This is ███████████████████████████████████████████
█████████████████████████████████████ I do not write this email
for my personal matter, but for some legal truth. Many young Ph.D.s in Taiwan like me are
playing Sherlock Holmes to crack the mystery of President Ing-wen Tsai's LSE Ph.D.
degree.

In this email, I attached a few Ms. Tsai's LSE documents (which she said provided by
LSE). However, these documents did not solve people's doubts about her LSE certificate
but aroused even more suspicion.

First of all, Ms. Tsai had three Ph.D. certificates that she obtained from 1984, 2010 and
2015 -- How come LSE issued her so many certificates at different times? Are they all
legitimate? My second question is, some important documents are lacking signatures of the
persons in charge -- Are these documents coming from LSE? Without signatures, are they
legitimate? (Attached documents are published by the President's spokesman on his FB
and in a press conference.)

I am very sorry if this email is bothering you or LSE, but this matter has caused much
disturbance in Taiwan's society in the past few months. Families and friends fought with
each other or broke off relations because of this. It has become it is either LSE's fault
(missing Ms. Tsai's thesis in three libraries, issuing documents without signatures, missing
details between 1983-84 in the student record) or it is Ms. Tsai's fault (if she did not follow
the right procedure to get her Ph.D. degree). How could she graduate without a principle
supervisor after 1982 as shown in the student record? (It is said that her supervisor Mr.
Michael Elliot left LSE in 1982.)

I am not in nature a political person. It is the first time that I care about a political issue so
much because it is related to academic dignity and truth. I realize it is not an easy matter.
All I can do is just writing this email.

Sincerely yours,
████████

# Re_ Ing-Wen Tsai's Ph.D. of 1984

| From: | Withers,IF |
|---|---|
| To: | Phdacademy |
| Cc: | Haynes,KJ; Metcalfe,F; Wilson,Clive; Thomson,MT |
| Subject: | Re: Ing-Wen Tsai"s PhD of 1984 |
| Date: | 03 October 2019 22:32:08 |

Hi Marcus

It seems appropriate to give some background and guidance to colleagues if we think more staff are being contacted, although do we have an idea of academic faculty likely to have been approached?

Happy to speak tomorrow to discuss and to also get Danny's expertise to make sure we are aligned with external comms.

Best wishes
Imogen

Sent from my IPhone

On 3 Oct 2019, at 21:55, LSE PhD Academy <phdacademy@lse.ac.uk> wrote:

> The one Kevin has attached has been sent to several people including the Simon Hix, Rita Astuti and Max Shulze. I have advised Rita to ignore but should we do some internal comms to academics likely to receive such queries?
>
> Thanks,
>
> Marcus
>
> **Marcus Cerny**
> **PhD Academy Deputy Director**
> The London School of Economics and Political Science
> Houghton Street, London WC2A 2AE
> t: +44 (0)20 7955 6766
> e: m.w.cerny@lse.ac.uk
> lse.ac.uk/phdacademy
>
> If you are a current PhD student please remember to send your queries through the PhD Academy Enquiry Form. All other enquirers should contact phdacademy@lse.ac.uk
>
> -------------- Original Message --------------
> **From:** Haynes,KJ [k.j.haynes@lse.ac.uk]
> **Sent:** 03/10/2019 16:24
> **To:** phdacademy@lse.ac.uk; m.t.thomson@lse.ac.uk; i.f.withers@lse.ac.uk
> **Cc:** clive.wilson@lse.ac.uk; f.metcalfe@lse.ac.uk; k.j.haynes@lse.ac.uk
> **Subject:** FW: Ing-Wen Tsai's PhD of 1984
>
> Hi Danny

I've attached another that you may already have seen. I think our party line more or less answers why we wouldn't be embarking on an investigation.

Best wishes, Kevin

LSE Legal Team

Secretary's Division

Room 3.01, 1 Kingsway

London School of Economics and Political Science

Houghton Street

London

WC2A 2AE

020 7955 7823

**From:** O'Connor,D
**Sent:** 03 October 2019 16:13
**To:** Phdacademy <Phdacademy@lse.ac.uk>; Thomson,MT <M.T.Thomson@lse.ac.uk>; Withers,IF <I.F.Withers@lse.ac.uk>
**Cc:** Wilson,Clive <CLIVE.Wilson@lse.ac.uk>; Metcalfe,F <F.Metcalfe@lse.ac.uk>; Haynes,KJ <K.J.Haynes@lse.ac.uk>
**Subject:** FW: Ing-Wen Tsai's PhD of 1984

Colleagues,

To note, the Director's office continue to receive emails from Hwan Lin.

I have advised against engaging with him at all. He has received a response from LSE on numerous occasions, and his subsequent allegations are weak and far-fetched.

Kind regards,

Danny

**From:** ███████████████████████████
**Sent:** 09 September 2019 03:29
**To:** Gajewska,M <M.Gajewska@lse.ac.uk>
**Subject:** Ing-Wen Tsai's PhD of 1984

Dear LSE Director Shafik:

I hope this email finds you well. I am writing to make inquiries about the authenticity of Ms. Tsai's LSE PhD in law, which, she claimed, was awarded in 1984. I am an academic economist in the US and I made my inquiries for the sake of academic honesty and integrity. As you may have noticed, Ms. Ing-Wen Tsai is President of Republic of China (Taiwan).

For your information, some new startling evidence just came up recently. On September 6, 2019, Ms. Ing-Wen Tsai's spokesperson displayed three documents in public in order to prove the authenticity of her so-called PhD in law. These documents are attached in this email for your review. To me, these documents instead prove that she was actually not awarded a PhD in 1984. My explanations of each document are in order:

#1. The first document is Ing-Wen Tsai's Student Records while she was a graduate student at LSE. This document clearly says that she was on a M. Phil. program between October, 1980 and November 10, 1982. In the entire course of study, she had two supervisors (Mr. Lazar and Mr. Elliott) for the academic year of 1980-81 and only one supervisor (Mr. Elliott) for the next academic year of 1981-82. The duration of the course of study was 21 months, much less than the duration of 3 - 4 years for a typical PhD program. The M. Phil program was clearly a master's program. Note that she withdrew from the course of study on November 10, 1982 for the sake of financial difficulties. All these are specified on the Student Records.

It is evident that she did not have any course of study at LSE starting from the day of November 10, 1982. But how could it be possible that the M. Phil program was later changed to a PhD program on the Student Records? And when was this change being made? For these questions, the Student Records provide no information at all. More absurd is that an undisclosed degree was awarded to her in February, 1984, which occurred about 16 months after she withdrew from the course of study. Moreover, the date of recording the degree-awarding event was about one year earlier than the occurrence of this event itself. How could one predict and record a far-away future event on Student Records?

Another serious problem is that the Student Records indicate nobody supervising Ing-Wen Tsai's doctoral study after she withdrew from the course of study on November 10, 1982. Even if we assume that Mr. Elliott continued to serve as Supervisor, it is still unbelievable that LSE could permit a bachelor-degree supervisor to direct a doctoral study. Note that Mr. Elliott graduated from Oxford University with a bachelor's degree and he was very young in the early 1980s. He left LSE in 1982 and joined the Central Policy Review Staff (CPRS) in 1983, which was the cabinet office's Think-Tank.

All these weird problems revealed that Ms. Tsai's Student Records are problematic and can never be a proof that she was awarded a PhD in 1984, given that she had not been an LSE student since November 10, 1982.

#2. The second document is a letter dated February 8, 1984 that Mrs. G. F. Roberts mailed to Ms. Ing-Wen Tsai's home address in Taipei, Taiwan. According to this letter, Mrs. G. F. Roberts was Academic Registrar from the University's Senate House. Ms. Tsai claimed that this letter was a proof that she passed her viva exam for a PhD. However, the letter did not mention the examination as a viva exam, and the two viva examiners were never mentioned at all in the letter and elsewhere, either. More seriously, Mrs. G. F. Roberts did not sign on the letter. Thus, how could such an unsigned letter be a formal proof of passing a viva exam for her PhD.

#3. The third document is a carbon copy of Ms. Tsai's so-called PhD diploma. According to Ms. Tsai, such a carbon copy was kept in the University of London and she got a copy of it from the University. Note that in the year of 2015, Ms. Tsai said that she applied for a replacement diploma from the University. She then displayed this replacement diploma in public on July 10, 2019. A month ago, an image file of this replacement was sent to you, as attached. According to the University's Head of Diploma Production Office, any replacement must be identical to the original diploma. However, the replacement that Ms. Tsai obtained in 2015 is totally different from the carbon copy of the so-called original diploma she obtained from the University. In other words, it is highly possible that the replacement is fake and came illegally from some unknown sources.

I was pulled into the investigation of Ms. Tsai's PhD diploma about three months ago when I tried to check out her thesis titled "Unfair Trade Practices

I was pulled into the investigation of Ms. Tsai's PhD diploma about three months ago when I tried to check out her thesis titled "Unfair Trade Practices

and Safeguard Actions" from LSE Library. The librarian told me that the University's Senate House Library had never received a copy of the thesis over the past 35 years, neither had the University's Institute of Advanced Legal Studies. This was a shock to me and then the investigation has since then continued.

On June 28, 2019, Ms. Tsai sent a facsimile copy of a so-called thesis to LSE Library for the first time in 35 years. It was bound into a hard-cover book and cataloged in the Library. This thesis then become searchable, starting from July 13, on the Library's online search system. On August 6 - 8, 2019, I visited LSE Library and reviewed this thesis. What shocked me was that I was not allowed to copy any part of the thesis's contents. You can see such illegal restrictions indicated on a white-colored paper band on the thesis, as attached. I found that the thesis has six missing pages in Chapter One (pages 5, 6, 7, 8, 9, 10 are missing) and its editorial checks and corrections were quite sloppy. It does not look like a PhD-level thesis.

After a three-month investigation, I have documented a 47-page report in Chinese, which is downloadable at my Facebook Page hwanclin. And an English-version of this report will be available soon. The report concludes that Ms. Ing-Wen Tsai was not awarded an LSE PhD in law in 1984.

I admire the global reputation of LSE. I sincerely hope that we all can work together to uphold the noble values of academic honesty and integrity. I believe that LSE would never compromise these values simply because Ms. Ing-Wen Tsai is President of Republic of China (Taiwan).

I hereby make a Freedom-of-Information-Act request that LSE should verify formally whether Ms. Ing-Wen Tsai was correctly awarded an LSE PhD in law in 1984.

Yours faithfully,

ref:_00D58JYzR._5004Itx0ND:ref

The biggest degree fraud case in human history

# RE_-Is-it-possible_-To-award-a-Ph.d.-degree-in-.1

| | |
|---|---|
| **From:** | O'Connor,D |
| **To:** | Metcalfe,F |
| **Subject:** | RE: Is it possible? To award a Ph.d. degree in Law without submission of the thesis? |
| **Date:** | 07 October 2019 13:49:00 |
| **Attachments:** | image002.png |
| | image003.png |
| | image005.png |

Seems fine, though they can't find a digital copy either!

Added a little more to the end.

**From:** Metcalfe,F
**Sent:** 07 October 2019 13:47
**To:** O'Connor,D <D.O'Connor@lse.ac.uk>
**Subject:** RE: Is it possible? To award a Ph.d. degree in Law without submission of the thesis?

Fair enough

What about

### LSE statement on PhD of Tsai Ing-wen

LSE has received a number of queries regarding the academic status of our alumna, Dr Tsai Ing-Wen, President of Taiwan.

We can be clear that the records of LSE and of the University of London - the degree awarding body at the time - confirm that Dr Ing-Wen was correctly awarded a PhD in Law in 1984.

All degrees from that period were awarded via the University of London and the thesis would have been sent first to their Senate House Library. However, it has recently been discovered that the University of London Senate House Library are unable to find the hard copy of the thesis.

The Senate House Library records confirm that a copy was received and sent by them to the Institute for Advanced Legal Studies (IALS) and there is a listing of Dr Ing-Wen's thesis 'Unfair trade practices and safeguard actions' In the IALS index document "Legal Research in the United Kingdom 1905-1984", which was published in 1985.

Dr Ing-wen recently provided the LSE Library with a facsimile of a personal copy of the thesis, *Unfair trade practices and safeguard actions* which is available to view in the Library Reading Room. We understand Dr Tsai has also provided a digital version of her personal copy to the National Central Library of Taiwan.

/END

Fiona Metcalfe
X2892

**From:** O'Connor,D
**Sent:** 07 October 2019 13:39
**To:** Metcalfe,F
**Subject:** RE: Is it possible? To award a Ph.d. degree in Law without submission of the thesis?

I think that's fine.

I don't know if we need to acknowledge that UoL did lose her original thesis.

**From:** Metcalfe,F
**Sent:** 07 October 2019 13:31
**To:** O'Connor,D <D.O'Connor@lse.ac.uk>
**Subject:** RE: Is it possible? To award a Ph.d. degree in Law without submission of the thesis?

What about this:

Fiona Metcalfe
X2892

**From:** O'Connor,D
**Sent:** 07 October 2019 12:58
**To:** Metcalfe,F
**Subject:** RE: Is it possible? To award a Ph.d. degree in Law without submission of the thesis?

Hey,

Have put together this for a web statement, I suspect it's too discursive but prefer to start long and then edit down.

D

## LSE statement on PhD of Tsai Ing-wen

LSE has received a number of queries regarding the academic status of our alumna, Dr Tsai Ing-Wen, President of Taiwan.

We can be clear that the records of LSE and of the University of London - the degree awarding body at the time - confirm that Dr Ing-Wen was correctly awarded a PhD in Law in 1984.

All degrees from that period were awarded via the University of London and the thesis would have been sent first to their Senate House Library.

The Senate House Library records confirm that a copy was received and sent by them to the Institute for Advanced Legal Studies (IALS) and there is a listing of Dr Ing-Wen's thesis 'Unfair trade practices and safeguard actions' In the IALS index document "Legal Research in the United Kingdown 1905-1984", which was published in 1985.

Dr Ing-wen recently provided the LSE Library with a facsimile of a personal copy of the thesis, *Unfair trade practices and safeguard actions* and has provided a digital copy to the National Central Library of Taiwan.

/END

**From:** Metcalfe,F
**Sent:** 07 October 2019 12:11
**To:** O'Connor,D <D.O'Connor@lse.ac.uk>
**Subject:** RE: Is it possible? To award a Ph.d. degree in Law without submission of the thesis?

I think we need to stop engaging

Can you put statement on website and only signpost
?

Fiona Metcalfe
X2892

**From:** O'Connor,D
**Sent:** 07 October 2019 11:38
**To:** Metcalfe,F
**Subject:** RE: Is it possible? To award a Ph.d. degree in Law without submission of the thesis?

Hi,

Does this seem ok to you? I realise I shouldn't be replying to all this stuff but it's sending me a bit insane.

Danny

Dear ▓▓▓▓▓▓▓▓▓▓,

I refer you back to our statement that the London School of Economics and Political Science and the University of London can confirm that Tsai Ing-Wen was correctly awarded a PhD in Law in 1984. The records of both institutions have been checked and both confirm this was correct.

With regards to your other questions: the School has received a number of emails from members of the public with false allegations about this issue. To avoid duplicate responses, the media relations office has been asked to collate and reply to many of these messages.

Thank you for the Wikipedia link but I am aware of the position of the Women's Library at LSE. You are, however, incorrect in your assertions. The dissertation is housed in LSE's central library catalogue. The Women's Library Reading Room (which is part of LSE) was used for those wishing to read it. [check with Clive]

As indicated in previous correspondence, this is a facsimile of the personal copy of Dr Tsai's thesis for those interested. The copy submitted for examination in 1980s could not be located by the University of London's Senate House.

We consider this matter closed.

Regards,

Daniel O'Connor

**From:** ▮▮▮▮▮▮▮▮▮▮▮▮▮▮▮▮▮▮▮▮▮▮▮▮
**Sent:** 07 October 2019 09:11
**To:** O'Connor,D <D.O'Connor@lse.ac.uk>
**Cc:** Media.Relations <Media.Relations@lse.ac.uk>; Carter,HC <H.C.Carter@lse.ac.uk>
**Subject:** Re: Is it possible? To award a Ph.d. degree in Law without submission of the thesis?

Dear Mr. O'Connor,

I am writing in relation to the following statement of your response dated 16th of September:

> ... For your information, Dr Tsai Ing-wen recently provided the LSE Library with a facsimile copy of the thesis, *Unfair trade practices and safeguard actions*. This is available to view in the LSE library reading room upon request.

Since it is not clear which LSE library you referred to that housed Ms. Tsai's thesis copy., I did some research and found it is housed at the LSE Women's Library.

I also found that Women's Library has been in the custody of the LSE, it is in fact not a formal LSE library that will house theses of LSE graduates.

For your information, below is a brief background information on the LSE Women's Library which was downloaded from Wikipedia:

" The **Women's Library @ LSE** is England's main library and museum resource on women and the women's movement, concentrating on Britain in the 19th and 20th centuries. It has an institutional history as a coherent collection dating back to the mid-1920s, although its "core" collection dates from a library established by Ruth Cavendish Bentinck in 1909. Since 2013, the library has been in the custody of the London School of Economics and Political Science (LSE), which manages the collection as part of the British Library of Political and Economic Science in a dedicated area known as the Women's Library @ LSE."

In view of the nature of the collections the Women's Library under the custody of LSE, the copy on Tsai's thesis displayed in LSE Women's Library is unlikely the one submitted to the

Law Department for the doctoral degree. The copy looks more like a personal collection. In addition, there were no signatures of the internal and external examiners.

Thank you for your attention.

Sincerely,

---

**From:**
**Sent:** Saturday, September 28, 2019 19:35
**To:** O'Connor,D <D.O'Connor@lse.ac.uk>
**Cc:** Media.Relations <Media.Relations@lse.ac.uk>; h.c.carter@lse.ac.uk <h.c.carter@lse.ac.uk>
**Subject:** Re: Is it possible? To award a Ph.d. degree in Law without submission of the thesis?

Dear Mr. O'Connor,

Thank you for your reply dated 16/09 my captioned query.

Having read your response, I have further questions which I will list below:

1. Why is it that Mrs. Carter from the Law Department cannot respond to me directly since it is obviously her job to know about Tsai's thesis in the Law Department.

2. Why should you in the Media/Communication Division respond to inquiries about LES's theses when it should be the responsibility of the relevant department such as the Law Department to do so where the theses are handled?

3. When was the copy of Tsai's thesis submitted? If it were in 1984, why there was no record of such; if it were in 2019, why?

4. Did LES award Tsai's degree based on the thesis in LES's Wemen's Library? If that is the case, then a whole series of questions raised by both Professor Lin of North Carolina and Dr. Xu, a ph.d. from Oxford U., can be asked as to why can LES accept a thesis like this-- sloppy format including different layout of the lines, corrections by hand, missing pages, no signatures of the advisers, etc.?

5. How can a thesis be without a conclusion at the end while in each chapter there is? Was this the common practice among the LES thesis awardees back in 1984?

Thank you.

Sincerely,

---

**From:** O'Connor,D <D.O'Connor@lse.ac.uk>
**Sent:** Monday, September 16, 2019 16:59
**To:**
**Cc:** Media.Relations <Media.Relations@lse.ac.uk>

158 The biggest degree fraud case in human history

**Subject:** RE: Is it possible? To award a Ph.d. degree in Law without submission of the thesis?

Dear ▮▮▮▮▮▮▮,

Thank you for your email to Ms Carter, I have been asked to respond.

As indicated to a number of enquirers, the London School of Economics and Political Science and the University of London can confirm categorically that Tsai Ing-Wen completed and submitted her thesis and was correctly awarded a PhD in Law in 1984.

For your information, Dr Tsai Ing-wen recently provided the LSE Library with a facsimile copy of the thesis, *Unfair trade practices and safeguard actions*. This is available to view in the LSE library reading room upon request.

Kind regards,

Daniel O'Connor

---

**Daniel O'Connor**
**Head of Media Relations | Communications Division**
The London School of Economics and Political Science
Houghton Street, London WC2A 2AE
t: +44 (0)20 7955 7417
e: oconnord@lse.ac.uk
lse.ac.uk

THE LONDON SCHOOL OF ECONOMICS AND POLITICAL SCIENCE

**LSE is ranked #1 in Europe for social sciences (QS World University Ranking 2019)**

---

**From:** ▮▮▮▮▮▮▮▮▮▮▮▮▮▮▮▮▮▮
**Sent:** 14 September 2019 08:41
**To:** Carter,HC
**Subject:** Fwd: Is it possible? To award a Ph.d. degree in Law without submission of the thesis?

Dear Madam,

Following my previous email message to you (attached below), I also enclose my university email address for your reference.

▮▮▮▮▮▮▮▮▮▮▮▮

Thank you.

The biggest degree fraud case in human history 159

Sincerely,

▮▮▮

---------- Forwarded message ---------
寄件者: ▮▮▮
Date: 2019年9月14日 週六 下午3:33
Subject: Is it possible? To award a Ph.d. degree in Law without submission of the thesis?
To: <h.c.carter@lse.ac.uk>

Dear Mrs. Carter,

Sorry to bother you about the captioned issue on the possibility of LSE Law Department awarding a ph.d. in law without submission of a ph.d. thesis.

My name is ▮▮▮ I am currently visiting my hometown in Taipei. As there will be a presidential election held in January 2020, potential voters are careful in examining the candidates. The issue on incumbent president Tsai Ing-wen who is seeking for a 2nd term in the coming election, is whether or not LSE law department awarded her a ph.d. degree in 1984, as she spent less than two years (1982-83) with LSE law department, and her ph.d. thesis was missing from the U of London library.

As this issue is in relation to a candidate's integrity, many of us, as valid voters, would like to seek clarification from your department on this issue.

The article attached below entitled "Tsai Ing-wen's missing thesis was not submitted says university library" raised questions on why the Law Department awarded Tsai a ph.d. degree in law without receiving her ph.d. thesis?

https://richardsonreports.wordpress.com/2019/07/04/tsai-ing-wens-missing-thesis-was-not-submitted-says-university-library/

As this issue has also become a most talk-about issues on local TV programs here in Taiwan.

Would be grateful if you could help resolve this puzzle.
Any exceptional case could happen?

Thank you very much for your time.

Sincerely yours,

▮▮▮

# RE_-Is-it-possible_-
# To-award-a-Ph.d.-degree-in-1-1

| From: | Wilson,Clive |
| --- | --- |
| To: | O"Connor,D |
| Subject: | RE: Is it possible? To award a Ph.d. degree in Law without submission of the thesis? |
| Date: | 07 October 2019 14:50:45 |
| Attachments: | image002.png |
| | image003.png |
| | image005.png |

Hi Danny

All of our theses, together with all unique or rare items, are housed within our Archives and Special Collections and can only be viewed in the Women's Library Reading Room. We are very proud to have named the reading room for the amazing collections that form the Women's Library but many other collections are also only viewable in that reading room: pamphlets, archived newspapers, papers and letters from many politicians, academics and organisations, maps, our extensive microfilm and fiche collections, to name but a few.

Feel free to rewrite that as you think appropriate. !

Clive

**From:** O'Connor,D
**Sent:** 07 October 2019 09:37
**To:** Wilson,Clive
**Subject:** FW: Is it possible? To award a Ph.d. degree in Law without submission of the thesis?

Hi Clive,

New conspiracy angle that it's housed in the Women's Library —

I'm not sure if it's worth a response but do let me know if there is any particular angle you'd want to highlight.

Danny

**From:** ███████████████████████████████
**Sent:** 07 October 2019 09:11
**To:** O'Connor,D <D.O'Connor@lse.ac.uk>
**Cc:** Media.Relations <Media.Relations@lse.ac.uk>; Carter,HC <H.C.Carter@lse.ac.uk>
**Subject:** Re: Is it possible? To award a Ph.d. degree in Law without submission of the thesis?

Dear Mr. O'Connor,

I am writing in relation to the following statement of your response dated 16th of September:

... For your information, Dr Tsai Ing-wen recently provided the LSE Library with a facsimile copy of the thesis, *Unfair trade practices and safeguard actions*. This is available to view in the LSE library reading room upon request.

Since it is not clear which LSE library you referred to that housed Ms. Tsai's thesis copy., I did some research and found it is housed at the LSE Women's Library.

I also found that Women's Library has been in the custody of the LSE, it is in fact not a formal LSE library that will house theses of LSE graduates.

For your information, below is a brief background information on the LSE Women's Library which was downloaded from Wikipedia:

" The **Women's Library @ LSE** is England's main library and museum resource on women and the women's movement, concentrating on Britain in the 19th and 20th centuries. It has an institutional history as a coherent collection dating back to the mid-1920s, although its "core" collection dates from a library established by Ruth Cavendish Bentinck in 1909. Since 2013, the library has been in the custody of the London School of Economics and Political Science (LSE), which manages the collection as part of the British Library of Political and Economic Science in a dedicated area known as the Women's Library @ LSE."

In view of the nature of the collections the Women's Library under the custody of LSE, the copy on Tsai's thesis displayed in LSE Women's Library is unlikely the one submitted to the Law Department for the doctoral degree. The copy looks more like a personal collection. In addition, there were no signatures of the internal and external examiners.

Thank you for your attention.

Sincerely,

███████████

---

**From:** ███████████████████████████████████
**Sent:** Saturday, September 28, 2019 19:35
**To:** O'Connor,D <D.O'Connor@lse.ac.uk>
**Cc:** Media.Relations <Media.Relations@lse.ac.uk>; h.c.carter@lse.ac.uk <h.c.carter@lse.ac.uk>
**Subject:** Re: Is it possible? To award a Ph.d. degree in Law without submission of the thesis?

Dear Mr. O'Connor,

Thank you for your reply dated 16/09 my captioned query.

Having read your response, I have further questions which I will list below:

1. Why is it that Mrs. Carter from the Law Department cannot respond to me directly since it is obviously her job to know about Tsai's thesis in the Law Department.

2. Why should you in the Media/Communication Division respond to inquiries about LES's theses when it should be the responsibility of the relevant department such as the Law Department to do so where the theses are handled?

3. When was the copy of Tsai's thesis submitted? If it were in 1984, why there was no record of such; if it were in 2019, why?

4. Did LES award Tsai's degree based on the thesis in LES's Women's Library? If that is the case, then a whole series of questions raised by both Professor Lin of North Carolina and Dr. Xu, a ph.d. from Oxford U., can be asked as to why can LES accept a thesis like this-- sloppy format including different layout of the lines, corrections by hand, missing pages, no signatures of the advisers, etc.?

5. How can a thesis be without a conclusion at the end while in each chapter there is? Was this the common practice among the LES thesis awardees back in 1984?

Thank you.

Sincerely,

██████████

**From:** O'Connor,D <D.O'Connor@lse.ac.uk>
**Sent:** Monday, September 16, 2019 16:59
**To:** ████████████████████████████████
**Cc:** Media.Relations <Media.Relations@lse.ac.uk>
**Subject:** RE: Is it possible? To award a Ph.d. degree in Law without submission of the thesis?

Dear ██████████,

Thank you for your email to Ms Carter, I have been asked to respond.

As indicated to a number of enquirers, the London School of Economics and Political Science and the University of London can confirm categorically that Tsai Ing-Wen completed and submitted her thesis and was correctly awarded a PhD in Law in 1984.

For your information, Dr Tsai Ing-wen recently provided the LSE Library with a facsimile copy of the thesis, *Unfair trade practices and safeguard actions*. This is available to view in the LSE library reading room upon request.

Kind regards,

Daniel O'Connor

**Daniel O'Connor**
**Head of Media Relations | Communications Division**
The London School of Economics and Political Science
Houghton Street, London WC2A 2AE
t: +44 (0)20 7955 7417
e: oconnord@lse.ac.uk
lse.ac.uk

**LSE** THE LONDON SCHOOL OF ECONOMICS AND POLITICAL SCIENCE

LSE is ranked #1 in Europe for social sciences
(QS World University Ranking 2019)

**From:** ▮▮▮▮▮▮▮▮▮▮▮▮▮▮▮
**Sent:** 14 September 2019 08:41
**To:** Carter,HC
**Subject:** Fwd: Is it possible? To award a Ph.d. degree in Law without submission of the thesis?

Dear Madam,

Following my previous email message to you (attached below), I also enclose my university email address for your reference.

▮▮▮▮▮▮▮▮▮▮▮▮▮▮▮

Thank you.

Sincerely,

▮▮▮▮▮▮▮▮▮▮

---------- Forwarded message ----------
寄件者: ▮▮▮▮▮▮▮▮▮▮▮▮▮▮▮
Date: 2019年9月14日 週六 下午3:33
Subject: Is it possible? To award a Ph.d. degree in Law without submission of the thesis?
To: <h.c.carter@lse.ac.uk>

Dear Mrs. Carter,

Sorry to bother you about the captioned issue on the possibility of LSE Law Department awarding a ph.d. in law without submission of a ph.d. thesis.

My name is ▮▮▮▮▮▮▮▮▮▮▮▮▮▮▮▮▮▮▮▮▮▮ I am currently visiting my hometown in Taipei. As there will be a presidential election held in January 2020, potential voters are careful in examining the candidates. The issue on incumbent president Tsai Ing-wen who is seeking for a 2nd term in the coming election, is whether or not LSE law department awarded her a ph.d. degree in 1984, as she spent less than two years (1982-83) with LSE law department, and her ph.d. thesis was missing from the U of London library.

As this issue is in relation to a candidate's integrity, many of us, as valid voters, would like

164 The biggest degree fraud case in human history

to seek clarification from your department on this issue.

The article attached below entitled "Tsai Ing-wen's missing thesis was not submitted says university library" raised questions on why the Law Department awarded Tsai a ph.d. degree in law without receiving her ph.d. thesis?

https://richardsonreports.wordpress.com/2019/07/04/tsai-ing-wens-missing-thesis-was-not-submitted-says-university-library/

As this issue has also become a most talk-about issues on local TV programs here in Taiwan.

Would be grateful if you could help resolve this puzzle.
Any exceptional case could happen?

Thank you very much for your time.

Sincerely yours,

# RE_ Report on President Tsai's degree

**From:** Haynes,KJ
**To:** Thomson,MT
**Subject:** RE: Report on President Tsai degree
**Date:** 01 October 2019 14:55:10

**From:** Thomson,MT
**Sent:** 01 October 2019 14:53
**To:** Haynes,KJ <K.J.Haynes@lse.ac.uk>
**Subject:** RE: Report on President Tsai degree

**From:** Haynes,KJ
**Sent:** 01 October 2019 14:52
**To:** O'Connor,D <D.O'Connor@lse.ac.uk>; Phdacademy <Phdacademy@lse.ac.uk>; Wilson,Clive <CLIVE.Wilson@lse.ac.uk>
**Cc:** Metcalfe,F <F.Metcalfe@lse.ac.uk>; Thomson,MT <M.T.Thomson@lse.ac.uk>; Withers,IF <I.F.Withers@lse.ac.uk>
**Subject:** RE: Report on President Tsai degree

HI

Sorry, this has been a spectator sport for me. I'd also let nature run its course if the thesis is now available online.

Best wishes, Kevin

LSE Legal Team
Secretary's Division
Room 3.01, 1 Kingsway
London School of Economics and Political Science
Houghton Street
London
WC2A 2AE

020 7955 7823

**From:** O'Connor,D
**Sent:** 01 October 2019 14:06
**To:** Phdacademy <Phdacademy@lse.ac.uk>; Wilson,Clive <CLIVE.Wilson@lse.ac.uk>
**Cc:** Metcalfe,F <F.Metcalfe@lse.ac.uk>; Haynes,KJ <K.J.Haynes@lse.ac.uk>; Thomson,MT <M.T.Thomson@lse.ac.uk>; Withers,IF <I.F.Withers@lse.ac.uk>
**Subject:** RE: Report on President Tsai degree

Thanks Marcus.

I realise the thesis is now available to view online via Taiwan's National Central Library, so hopefully this will reduce some of the nonsense.

Danny

**From:** LSE PhD Academy [mailto:phdacademy@lse.ac.uk]
**Sent:** 01 October 2019 13:43
**To:** Wilson,Clive <CLIVE.Wilson@lse.ac.uk>
**Cc:** Metcalfe,F <F.Metcalfe@lse.ac.uk>; O'Connor,D <D.O'Connor@lse.ac.uk>; Haynes,KJ <K.J.Haynes@lse.ac.uk>; Thomson,MT <M.T.Thomson@lse.ac.uk>; Withers,IF <I.F.Withers@lse.ac.uk>
**Subject:** RE: Report on President Tsai degree

Thanks Danny,

I have read it and it doesn't raise anything new in terms of issues relating to the School, University, IALTS etc. to which we have already responded. However, the addition of personal accusations of lying against identified individuals is something we haven't responded to and we should keep an eye on this to make sure that these are addressed if necessary.

Marcus

**Marcus Cerny**
**PhD Academy Deputy Director**
The London School of Economics and Political Science
Houghton Street, London WC2A 2AE
t: +44 (0)20 7955 6766
e: m.w.cerny@lse.ac.uk
lse.ac.uk/phdacademy

If you are a current PhD student please remember to send your queries through the PhD Academy Enquiry Form. All other enquirers should contact phdacademy@lse.ac.uk

--------------- Original Message ---------------
**From:** Wilson,Clive [clive.wilson@lse.ac.uk]
**Sent:** 01/10/2019 12:26
**To:** m.t.thomson@lse.ac.uk; phdacademy@lse.ac.uk; d.o'connor@lse.ac.uk; k.j.haynes@lse.ac.uk
**Cc:** f.metcalfe@lse.ac.uk; i.f.withers@lse.ac.uk
**Subject:** RE: Report on President Tsai degree

One hopes his own doctoral research was of a higher standard than this report ...
Clive

**From:** O'Connor,D
**Sent:** 01 October 2019 12:24
**To:** Phdacademy; Thomson,MT; Haynes,KJ
**Cc:** Metcalfe,F; Wilson,Clive; Withers,IF
**Subject:** RE: Report on President Tsai degree

Just to add, this was shared by a contact in the Taiwanese Govt who has been in touch with Clive.

Regards,

Danny

**From:** O'Connor,D
**Sent:** 01 October 2019 12:23
**To:** Phdacademy <Phdacademy@lse.ac.uk>; Thomson,MT <M.T.Thomson@lse.ac.uk>; Haynes,KJ <K.J.Haynes@lse.ac.uk>
**Cc:** Metcalfe,F <F.Metcalfe@lse.ac.uk>; Wilson,Clive <CLIVE.Wilson@lse.ac.uk>; Withers,IF (I.F.Withers@lse.ac.uk) <I.F.Withers@lse.ac.uk>
**Subject:** Report on President Tsai degree

Dear colleagues,

For information, please see attached an English translation of the report by ▮▮▮▮▮▮ against Tsai and LSE, claiming LSE is illegally covering up for President Tsai regarding the PhD matter.

I haven't read it fully - It is long, rambling, incoherent and moves from Gaddafi to accusations against Fang-long and to repeated accusations that I am "lying", among other things.

*(Page 40) "This public relations head Mr. D.O. stated: the 'records' of both the LSE and the University of London confirm that Tsai Ing-Wen received a Ph.D. in Law in 1984, and the student record shows Tsai had submitted the dissertation. Obviously this public relations head is lying!"*

*(p 42) "This investigation's search results proves that the LSE Research Support Services' library assistant Ms. R.O. was correct, and that LSE public relations head Mr. D.O. was clearly attempting to lie and cover up for Tsai Ing-Wen."*

*Plus (p43, p 44)*

As frustrating as this is, I am not sure it'll do much good to start issuing detailed denials, or to engage with ▮▮▮▮. He seemed to be a somewhat vindictive individual throughout the process.

(Kevin FYI - you probably haven't seen much of this but there is a conspiracy theory going round parts of Taiwan that the President never got her PhD from LSE).

Kind regards,

Danny

**From:** Wilson,Clive
**Sent:** 01 October 2019 09:44
**To:** O'Connor,D <D.O'Connor@lse.ac.uk>
**Subject:** FW: English version of Lin's report

Hi Danny

FYI. I haven't read it yet, won't have time until later, but if you think anyone else needs to see it please do pass it on.

I'm sure it will just make me cross!!

Clive

**From:** ▉▉▉▉▉▉▉▉▉▉▉▉▉▉▉▉
**Sent:** 01 October 2019 09:24
**To:** Wilson,Clive
**Subject:** English version of Lin's report

Hi Clive,

I would like to share the English version of ▉▉ report with you. ▉▉ accusation of LSE begins from page 26, which I believe is quite ridiculous.
Please let me know what you have in mind about this.

Many thanks,
▉▉

ref:_00D58JYzR._5004Itwd3V:ref

# RE_ Report on President Tsai's degree (2)

**To:** Phdacademy; Thomson,MT; Haynes,KJ
**Cc:** Metcalfe,F; Wilson,Clive; Withers,IF
**Subject:** RE: Report on President Tsai degree
**Date:** 01 October 2019 13:41:46

Hi all,

Further to this, a few more relevant points.

Tsai Ing-wen's thesis is now available to download from the Taiwanese National Central library.

███████████ report is from the end of August...so has moved on somewhat now.

This makes me think any

**From:** O'Connor,D
**Sent:** 01 October 2019 12:24
**To:** Phdacademy <Phdacademy@lse.ac.uk>; Thomson,MT <M.T.Thomson@lse.ac.uk>; Haynes,KJ <K.J.Haynes@lse.ac.uk>
**Cc:** Metcalfe,F <F.Metcalfe@lse.ac.uk>; Wilson,Clive <CLIVE.Wilson@lse.ac.uk>; Withers,IF (I.F.Withers@lse.ac.uk) <I.F.Withers@lse.ac.uk>
**Subject:** RE: Report on President Tsai degree

Just to add, this was shared by a contact in the Taiwanese Govt who has been in touch with Clive.

Regards,
Danny

**From:** O'Connor,D
**Sent:** 01 October 2019 12:23
**To:** Phdacademy <Phdacademy@lse.ac.uk>; Thomson,MT <M.T.Thomson@lse.ac.uk>; Haynes,KJ <K.J.Haynes@lse.ac.uk>
**Cc:** Metcalfe,F <F.Metcalfe@lse.ac.uk>; Wilson,Clive <CLIVE.Wilson@lse.ac.uk>; Withers,IF (I.F.Withers@lse.ac.uk) <I.F.Withers@lse.ac.uk>
**Subject:** Report on President Tsai degree

Dear colleagues,

For information, please see attached an English translation of the report by ███████████ against Tsai and LSE, claiming LSE is illegally covering up for President Tsai regarding the PhD matter.

I haven't read it fully - It is long, rambling, incoherent and moves from Gaddafi to accusations against Fang-long and to repeated accusations that I am "lying", among other things.

> (Page 40) "This public relations head Mr. D.O. stated: the 'records' of both the LSE and the University of London confirm that Tsai Ing-Wen received a Ph.D. in Law in 1984, and the student

record shows Tsai had submitted the dissertation. Obviously this public relations head is lying!"

(p 42) "This investigation's search results proves that the LSE Research Support Services' library assistant Ms. R.O. was correct, and that LSE public relations head Mr. D.O. was clearly attempting to lie and cover up for Tsai Ing-Wen."

Plus (p43, p 44)

As frustrating as this is, I am not sure it'll do much good to start issuing detailed denials, or to engage with ▮. He seemed to be a somewhat vindictive individual throughout the process.

(Kevin FYI - you probably haven't seen much of this but there is a conspiracy theory going round parts of Taiwan that the President never got her PhD from LSE).

Kind regards,

Danny

---

**From:** Wilson, Clive
**Sent:** 01 October 2019 09:44
**To:** O'Connor,D <D.O'Connor@lse.ac.uk>
**Subject:** FW: English version of Lin's report

Hi Danny

FYI. I haven't read it yet, won't have time until later, but if you think anyone else needs to see it please do pass it on.

I'm sure it will just make me cross!!

Clive

---

**From:** ▮
**Sent:** 01 October 2019 09:24
**To:** Wilson, Clive
**Subject:** English version of Lin's report

Hi Clive,

I would like to share the English version of ▮ report with you ▮ accusation of LSE begins from page 26, which I believe is quite ridiculous.
Please let me know what you have in mind about this.

Many thanks,
▮

恶官 3

# LSE's Strategy in the Face of Scrutiny: Blame it on Fake Accounts!

# LSE's Strategy in the Face of Scrutiny: Blame it on Fake Accounts!

Upon receiving external inquiries about the viva, O'Connor decided to forward the letter to Rachael Maguire, Records Manager at LSE, in hopes of refusing to answer.

Meanwhile, another letter landed in his inbox. This one was from someone hoping that LSE's statement could also be disseminated via the School of Advanced Study website at the University of London. O'Connor saw this as an excellent opportunity to garner more support for LSE's stance.

However, things could have been more straightforward. After meeting with a mysterious figure, O'Connor decided to amend the statement. He was concerned that the statement was too 'circulated,' which could provoke even more significant controversy. Thus, he collaborated with Wilson to assist the Taiwan Presidential Office smuggle the thesis.

But as the adage goes, one lie leads to another. When the statement mentioned that the University of London had a copy of Tsai's thesis, the outside world questioned its cataloging number at its alleged inclusion. Representatives from the Taiwan Presidential Office, including Shih, unapologetically hoped that LSE could assist in 'adding' a catalog number to quell external doubts.

The legal department at LSE suggested that the statement include more links to assert LSE's position more strongly. However, O'Connor was firmly against this idea. He believed it would only complicate matters further.

At this point, Taiwanese lawyer Tung Wen-hsun joined the accusation, charging Tsai with self-plagiarizing a 1983 Chinese journal and stating that her New York bar qualification had been suspended. LSE's higher-ups scoffed at the accusations, suggesting that the complainants were just individuals intent on making provocative comments to incite others.

Faced with relentless external questioning, LSE decided to respond with a statement. They adopted a stern tone and even accused outsiders of attacking them with fake accounts. They resolved to handle these issues using the Freedom of Information Act.

Before issuing the statement, LSE chose to inform Shih first. They hoped to secure her support.

As for Professor Peng's vow to initiate a lawsuit, LSE remained silent. They were aware that this academic storm was far from over.

# RE_ Request for information (4)

**From:** Donnelly,S
**To:** O"Connor,D; Maguire,RE
**Subject:** RE: Request for information
**Date:** 03 October 2019 10:25:46
**Attachments:** image002.png
image003.png
image005.png
image006.png

I'll check the file later today and see what information we actually have – as this is a University of London degree.

Sue

**Sue Donnelly**
**LSE Archivist | Secretary's Division**
The London School of Economics and Political Science
Houghton Street, London WC2A 2AE
t: +44 (0)20 3486 2840
e: s.donnelly@lse.ac.uk
lse.ac.uk

LSE is ranked #1 in Europe for social sciences
(QS World University Ranking 2018)

**From:** O'Connor,D
**Sent:** 03 October 2019 10:14
**To:** Maguire,RE <R.E.Maguire@lse.ac.uk>; Donnelly,S <S.Donnelly@lse.ac.uk>
**Subject:** RE: Request for information

Thanks Rachael.

I am minded to say that a lot of this information is restricted under Data protection....but – as you suggest - it may be that Tsai herself wants the information to come out.

Danny

**From:** Maguire,RE
**Sent:** 03 October 2019 10:05
**To:** Donnelly,S <S.Donnelly@lse.ac.uk>
**Cc:** O'Connor,D <D.O'Connor@lse.ac.uk>
**Subject:** RE: Request for information

Hello Sue,

My comments are below.

The biggest degree fraud case in human history 175

Rachael

**From:** Donnelly,S
**Sent:** 03 October 2019 09:55
**To:** Maguire,RE <R.E.Maguire@lse.ac.uk>
**Subject:** FW: Request for information


**From:** O'Connor,D
**Sent:** 03 October 2019 09:49
**To:** Cerny,MW <M.W.Cerny@lse.ac.uk>; Donnelly,S <S.Donnelly@lse.ac.uk>; Thomson,MT <M.T.Thomson@lse.ac.uk>
**Cc:** Wilson,Clive <CLIVE.Wilson@lse.ac.uk>
**Subject:** FW: Request for information

Dear all,

(See below) This individual is one of the main characters stirring up this story.

His blog is effectively the main English-language outlet for the conspiracy theory.

While I don't want to keep doing a back-and-forth can we answer these questions in a dry factual way (if data protection etc. allows).

(We may be able to put this to our FoI team as well go be clear on the 20-day response time).

Danny

Begin forwarded message:

**From:** ███████████████████████
**Date:** 2 October 2019 at 23:56:14 BST
**To:** j.winterstein@lse.ac.uk
**Subject: Request for information**

I am working on an article about the controversy surrounding Republic of China in-exile President Tsai Ing-wen's LSE graduate thesis. Ms. Tsai filed her 1984 theis with the LSE Library in 2019 and that has generated much public interest in Taiwan. The name of the thesis is "Unfair Trade Practices and Safeguard Actions."

My questions, for publication, are:

1) What is the name and degree of Tsai Ing-wen's LSE Advisor? – As he is deceased, this is no longer covered by data protection, so can be released.
2) What are the names of the thesis Examiners? - We normally do not release examiner names under any circumstances. However, considering the situation, it's whether there would be any harm to the examiners from releasing this information. If they are deceased,

1) **What is the name and degree of Tsai Ing-wen's LSE Advisor?** – As he is deceased, this is no longer covered by data protection, so can be released.
2) **What are the names of the thesis Examiners?** - We normally do not release examiner names under any circumstances. However, considering the situation, it's whether there would be any harm to the examiners from releasing this information. If they are deceased, it's the same situation as for the supervisor. If they are retired, there is unlikely to be any harm to their careers, but intense media interest could come their way. If they are still working, there could be potential harm to their careers due to intense media interest. To summarise, assuming we hold this info and not UoL, if the examiners are dead – release the names. If they are not – don't release the names as this could bring them under media interest that would be out of all proportion to the role they played. This would fit under the Section 40(2) exemption.
3) **What is the date of the thesis oral review?** – Could be released, it's personal data but it is in Ms Tsai's interests that we confirm the review.
4) **What is the date of the Examiner's signatures of approval?** - Could be released, it's personal data but it is in Ms Tsai's interests that we confirm the approval.

If you are not the correct person to handle this information request please forward to the appropriate individual.

Thank you for your attention to this request.

# RE_ Statement on LSE website

**From:** O"Connor,D
**To:** ▮
**Cc:**
**Subject:** RE: Statement on LSE website
**Date:** 10 October 2019 09:45:00

Dear colleagues,

This has now been posted: http://www.lse.ac.uk/News/Latest-news-from-LSE/2019/j-October-2019/LSE-statement-on-PhD-of-Dr-Tsai-Ing-wen

Best wishes,
Danny

**From:** ▮
**Sent:** 10 October 2019 09:31
**To:** O'Connor,D <D.O'Connor@lse.ac.uk>; ▮
**Subject:** RE: Statement on LSE website

Dear All,

Just to let you know that the LSE are proposing to post the statement below on their website, if it hasn't already been posted. Danny from the LSE press office, and I have been through the pros and cons on this. I recognise the need for the LSE to do this and I am happy with this as the final version.

I have copied Danny into this email to confirm whether or not it has been posted and perhaps we could have a link to it?

▮ in SAS is off, not sure who else to send it to in SAS – ▮ can you help with this please?

In the meantime, any enquiries on this matter at our end, please continue to refer them to me.
I am on leave today and tomorrow. If anything urgent comes up please feel free to call or email me.

Many thanks

## LSE statement on PhD of Dr Tsai Ing-wen

LSE has received a number of queries regarding the academic status of our alumna, Dr Tsai Ing-wen, President of Taiwan.

We can be clear the records of LSE and of the University of London - the degree awarding body at the time - confirm that Dr Tsai was correctly awarded a PhD in Law in 1984.

All degrees from that period were awarded via the University of London and the thesis would have been sent first to their Senate House Library.

The Senate House Library records confirm that a copy was received and sent by them to the Institute for Advanced Legal Studies (IALS). There is a listing of Dr Tsai's thesis 'Unfair trade practices and safeguard actions' in the IALS index document "Legal Research in the United Kingdom 1905-1984", which was published in 1985.

Dr Tsai recently provided the LSE Library with a facsimile of a personal copy of the thesis, Unfair trade practices and safeguard actions which is available to view in the Library Reading Room. We understand Dr Tsai has also provided a digital version of her personal copy to the National Central Library of Taiwan.

# Re_ Statement for the LSE website (1)

**From:** Donnelly,S
**To:** Phdacademy; Wilson,Clive
**Cc:** Metcalfe,F; Media.Relations; O"Connor,D; Thomson,MT; Comms.Socialmedia
**Subject:** Re: Statement for the LSE website
**Date:** 08 October 2019 17:10:28
**Attachments:** image002.png
image003.png
image005.png

That's fine with me

Sue

Sent from my Samsung Galaxy smartphone. Kk

-------- Original message --------
From: LSE PhD Academy <phdacademy@lse.ac.uk>
Date: 08/10/2019 16:34 (GMT+00:00)
To: "Wilson,Clive" <CLIVE.Wilson@lse.ac.uk>
Cc: "Metcalfe,F" <F.Metcalfe@lse.ac.uk>, "Media.Relations" <Media.Relations@lse.ac.uk>, "O'Connor,D" <D.O'Connor@lse.ac.uk>, "Thomson,MT" <M.T.Thomson@lse.ac.uk>, "Donnelly,S" <S.Donnelly@lse.ac.uk>, "Comms.Socialmedia" <Comms.Socialmedia@lse.ac.uk>
Subject: RE: Statement for the LSE website

Happy for that to be deleted.

Thanks,

Marcus

**Marcus Cerny**
**PhD Academy Deputy Director**
The London School of Economics and Political Science
Houghton Street, London WC2A 2AE
t: +44 (0)20 7955 6766
e: m.w.cerny@lse.ac.uk
lse.ac.uk/phdacademy

If you are a current PhD student please remember to send your queries through the PhD Academy Enquiry Form. All other enquirers should contact phdacademy@lse.ac.uk

--------------- Original Message ---------------
**From:** Wilson,Clive [clive.wilson@lse.ac.uk]
**Sent:** 08/10/2019 16:10
**To:** phdacademy@lse.ac.uk; d.o'connor@lse.ac.uk
**Cc:** f.metcalfe@lse.ac.uk; m.t.thomson@lse.ac.uk; s.donnelly@lse.ac.uk; media.relations@lse.ac.uk; comms.socialmedia@lse.ac.uk

**Subject:** RE: Statement for the LSE website

☺ no worries

**From:** O'Connor,D
**Sent:** 08 October 2019 16:10
**To:** Wilson,Clive; Phdacademy
**Cc:** Metcalfe,F; Thomson,MT; Donnelly,S; Media.Relations; Comms.Socialmedia
**Subject:** RE: Statement for the LSE website

Thanks Clive.

I understand the reasoning but I think that might just add to the confusion.

**From:** Wilson,Clive
**Sent:** 08 October 2019 16:03
**To:** O'Connor,D <D.O'Connor@lse.ac.uk>; Phdacademy <Phdacademy@lse.ac.uk>
**Cc:** Metcalfe,F <F.Metcalfe@lse.ac.uk>; Thomson,MT <M.T.Thomson@lse.ac.uk>; Donnelly,S <S.Donnelly@lse.ac.uk>; Media.Relations <Media.Relations@lse.ac.uk>; Comms.Socialmedia <Comms.Socialmedia@lse.ac.uk>
**Subject:** RE: Statement for the LSE website

Hi Danny

that sounds fine to me. But just thinking aloud - if that sentence comes out, do we want to add 'Although many students did, there was no requirement to submit a second copy to LSE Library'

Clive

**From:** O'Connor,D
**Sent:** 08 October 2019 15:19
**To:** Phdacademy
**Cc:** Metcalfe,F; Wilson,Clive; Thomson,MT; Donnelly,S; Media.Relations; Comms.Socialmedia

**Subject:** RE: Statement for the LSE website

Dear all,

███████████████████ The University of London is quite concerned by the statement, specifically this part

*"However, it has recently been discovered that the University of London Senate House Library are unable to find the hard copy of the thesis."*

**Would colleagues object if this sentence was just deleted?** On reflection, it doesn't seem to impact the overall message.

Best wishes,

Danny

**From:** O'Connor,D
**Sent:** 08 October 2019 13:39
**To:** LSE PhD Academy <phdacademy@lse.ac.uk>
**Cc:** Metcalfe,F <F.Metcalfe@lse.ac.uk>; Wilson,Clive <CLIVE.Wilson@lse.ac.uk>; Thomson,MT <M.T.Thomson@lse.ac.uk>; Donnelly,S <S.Donnelly@lse.ac.uk>; Media.Relations <Media.Relations@lse.ac.uk>; Comms.Socialmedia <Comms.Socialmedia@lse.ac.uk>
**Subject:** RE: Statement for the LSE website

Dear all,

The statement is live here: http://www.lse.ac.uk/News/Latest-news-from-LSE/2019/j-October-2019/LSE-statement-on-PhD-of-Dr-Tsai-Ing-wen

Media/ social media colleagues – this is a statement on President Tsai's PhD on our website.

Best wishes,

Danny

**From:** LSE PhD Academy [mailto:phdacademy@lse.ac.uk]
**Sent:** 08 October 2019 10:26
**To:** O'Connor,D <D.O'Connor@lse.ac.uk>
**Cc:** Metcalfe,F <F.Metcalfe@lse.ac.uk>; Wilson,Clive <CLIVE.Wilson@lse.ac.uk>; Thomson,MT <M.T.Thomson@lse.ac.uk>; Donnelly,S <S.Donnelly@lse.ac.uk>
**Subject:** RE: Statement for the LSE website

That looks good to me. If everybody else agrees let me know when and where it is up and I'll respond to queries directing to this.

I will also contact the Law Dept and those that have sent on queries to me to let them know. Do we need to do anything else via internal comms so that people are aware? It is hard to guess who exactly might receive a random query.

Thanks,
Marcus

**Marcus Cerny**
**PhD Academy Deputy Director**
The London School of Economics and Political Science
Houghton Street, London WC2A 2AE
t: +44 (0)20 7955 6766
e: m.w.cerny@lse.ac.uk
lse.ac.uk/phdacademy

If you are a current PhD student please remember to send your queries through the PhD Academy Enquiry Form. All other enquirers should contact phdacademy@lse.ac.uk

--------------- Original Message ---------------
**From:** O'Connor,D [d.o'connor@lse.ac.uk]
**Sent:** 08/10/2019 09:35
**To:** phdacademy@lse.ac.uk; m.t.thomson@lse.ac.uk
**Cc:** clive.wilson@lse.ac.uk; f.metcalfe@lse.ac.uk; s.donnelly@lse.ac.uk
**Subject:** Statement for the LSE website

Dear colleagues,

Further to the correspondence yesterday, Fiona and I have put together a draft statement (below) which can go on the LSE website. It is based on previously agreed statements and deliberately does not go into the range of claims and counter-claims being circulated

**Please let me know if there is anything of concern or anything you believe needs to be added/ deleted.**

Ideally we would like to get this uploaded later today.

Best wishes,

Danny

## LSE statement on PhD of Tsai Ing-wen

LSE has received a number of queries regarding the academic status of our alumna, Dr Tsai Ing-Wen, President of Taiwan.

We can be clear that the records of LSE and of the University of London - the degree awarding body at the time - confirm that Dr Ing-Wen was correctly awarded a PhD in Law in 1984.

All degrees from that period were awarded via the University of London and the thesis would have been sent first to their Senate House Library.

The Senate House Library records confirm that a copy was received and sent by them to the Institute for Advanced Legal Studies (IALS) and there is a listing of Dr Ing-Wen's thesis 'Unfair trade practices and safeguard actions' In the IALS index document "Legal Research in the United Kingdown 1905-1984", which was published in 1985.

Dr Ing-wen recently provided the LSE Library with a facsimile of a personal copy of the thesis, *Unfair trade practices and safeguard actions* which is available to view in the Library Reading Room. We understand Dr Tsai has also provided a digital version of her personal copy to the National Central Library of Taiwan.

/END

Daniel O'Connor

Head of Media Relations | Communications Division

The London School of Economics and Political Science

Houghton Street, London WC2A 2AE

t: +44 (0)20 7955 7417

e: oconnord@lse.ac.uk

lse.ac.uk

**LSE is ranked #1 in Europe for social sciences**

**(QS World University Ranking 2019)**

ref:_00D58JYzR._5004ItxPeD:ref

# RE_ Statement for the LSE website (8)

**From:** O"Connor,D
**To:** Wilson,Clive; Phdacademy; Thomson,MT
**Cc:** Donnelly,S; Metcalfe,F
**Subject:** RE: Statement for the LSE website
**Date:** 08 October 2019 10:16:54
**Attachments:** image002.png
image003.png
image005.png

Good spot Clive.

I think it's ok to make available as electronic copy though inevitably we'll be asked a flurry of questions about the process behind this.

Danny

**From:** Wilson,Clive
**Sent:** 08 October 2019 10:04
**To:** O'Connor,D <D.O'Connor@lse.ac.uk>; Phdacademy <Phdacademy@lse.ac.uk>; Thomson,MT <M.T.Thomson@lse.ac.uk>
**Cc:** Donnelly,S <S.Donnelly@lse.ac.uk>; Metcalfe,F <F.Metcalfe@lse.ac.uk>
**Subject:** RE: Statement for the LSE website

Hi Danny (and everyone)

I still get confused as to the correct way to address people and whether it should be Tsai Ing-Wen or Ing-Wen Tsai, but Tsai is the family name so it should be Dr Tsai in the 2$^{nd}$ line.

I was given permission from her office yesterday to upload the electronic copy.  If we host it on LSE theses online, it also means we can revert to the 'normal' copyright statement on the print copy.   Uploading copy from it will still be illegal, but if it's online anyway that is less of an issue.   It might mitigate some of the 'unreasonable restrictions' emails.

We will still describe it as a copy …

thanks

Clive

**From:** O'Connor,D
**Sent:** 08 October 2019 09:36
**To:** Phdacademy; Thomson,MT
**Cc:** Wilson,Clive; Donnelly,S; Metcalfe,F
**Subject:** Statement for the LSE website

Dear colleagues,

Further to the correspondence yesterday, Fiona and I have put together a draft statement (below) which can go on the LSE website. It is based on previously agreed statements and deliberately does not go into the range of claims and counter-claims being circulated

**Please let me know if there is anything of concern or anything you believe needs to be added/ deleted.**

Ideally we would like to get this uploaded later today.

Best wishes,

Danny

## LSE statement on PhD of Tsai Ing-wen

LSE has received a number of queries regarding the academic status of our alumna, Dr Tsai Ing-Wen, President of Taiwan.

We can be clear that the records of LSE and of the University of London - the degree awarding body at the time - confirm that Dr Ing-Wen was correctly awarded a PhD in Law in 1984.

All degrees from that period were awarded via the University of London and the thesis would have been sent first to their Senate House Library. However, it has recently been discovered that the University of London Senate House Library are unable to find the hard copy of the thesis.

The Senate House Library records confirm that a copy was received and sent by them to the Institute for Advanced Legal Studies (IALS) and there is a listing of Dr Ing-Wen's thesis 'Unfair trade practices and safeguard actions' In the IALS index document "Legal Research in the United Kingdom 1905-1984", which was published in 1985.

Dr Ing-wen recently provided the LSE Library with a facsimile of a personal copy of the thesis, *Unfair trade practices and safeguard actions* which is available to view in the Library Reading Room. We understand Dr Tsai has also provided a digital version of her personal copy to the National Central Library of Taiwan.

/END

**Daniel O'Connor**
**Head of Media Relations | Communications Division**
The London School of Economics and Political Science
Houghton Street, London WC2A 2AE
t: +44 (0)20 7955 7417
e: oconnord@lse.ac.uk
lse.ac.uk

LSE is ranked #1 in Europe for social sciences
(QS World University Ranking 2019)

# Re_-Statement-on-the-LSE-website1

| | |
|---|---|
| **From:** | O"Connor,D |
| **To:** | Fang-Long Shih |
| **Subject:** | Re: Statement on the LSE website |
| **Date:** | 09 October 2019 10:43:14 |

Hi Fang-long,

Thanks for your email, though I haven't got a new job!

I'll ask library colleagues about the catelogue number.

Best wishes,
Danny

**From:** Fang-Long Shih <fgshih@gmail.com>
**Sent:** 09 October 2019 05:12
**To:** O'Connor,D <D.O'Connor@lse.ac.uk>
**Subject:** Statement on the LSE website

Dear Danny,
Congratulations to your new position as Head of Media Relations and Communications Division!
It is a good idea to put a statement on the LSE website. Thank you for drafting this statement which looks good.
However, if U of London's Senate House Library still keeps its original paper version of the "book-search index cards" before the library collections became digitized? If so, whether there was a catalogue number assigned to the original thesis copy by the Senate House Library when the thesis was submitted?
It is believed if one can locate the catalogue number assigned to the original thesis, it's the exact proof that President Tsai completed the process. One can no longer cast any further doubt. As to what happened to the submitted copy (even missing), it's another story.

Do you think if you could assist to find and add this catalogue number? Many thanks!
I am currently in Seattle and will fly to Taiwan in 4 hours for an intensive international course until 17 Oct, and then will teach in Masaryk University in Czech and be back in London on 28 October. If I could help do anything while I am here, please don't hesitate to let me know.
All the very best,
Fang-long

# RE_ Status of Media Relations request

**From:** O'Connor,D
**To:** GLPD.Info.Rights; Winterstein,J
**Cc:** Metcalfe,F
**Subject:** RE: Status of Media Relations request
**Date:** 10 October 2019 10:44:00

Hi Rachael,

I understand the reasoning but I really don't want to add anything more to the statement.

Every time we give a bit more info, they just come back with more questions.

We have to draw the line somewhere.

Thanks,
Danny

(Fiona, FYI)

**From:** GLPD.Info.Rights
**Sent:** 10 October 2019 10:38
**To:** O'Connor,D <D.O'Connor@lse.ac.uk>; Winterstein,J <J.Winterstein@lse.ac.uk>
**Subject:** RE: Status of Media Relations request

Hello Danny,

A common thread to the questions are the names and dates. Can we add these to the statement please?

I was hoping we'd had a request through What Do They Know we could link to but no luck there.

Regards,
Rachael

**From:** O'Connor,D
**Sent:** 10 October 2019 10:34
**To:** GLPD.Info.Rights <GLPD.Info.Rights@lse.ac.uk>; Winterstein,J <J.Winterstein@lse.ac.uk>
**Subject:** RE: Status of Media Relations request

Hi Rachael,

It's on the website now.

http://www.lse.ac.uk/News/Latest-news-from-LSE/2019/j-October-2019/LSE-statement-on-PhD-of-Dr-Tsai-Ing-wen

Though it doesn't address his specific questions.

Best wishes,

Danny

**From:** GLPD.Info.Rights
**Sent:** 10 October 2019 10:32
**To:** Winterstein,J <J.Winterstein@lse.ac.uk>
**Cc:** O'Connor,D <D.O'Connor@lse.ac.uk>

**Subject:** FW: Status of Media Relations request

Hello Jess,

Do we know when the statement will be on the School's website yet?

Regards,
Rachael

**From:** ▮▮▮▮▮▮▮▮▮▮▮▮▮▮▮▮▮▮▮▮▮
**Sent:** 10 October 2019 03:18
**To:** GLPD.Info.Rights <GLPD.Info.Rights@lse.ac.uk>
**Cc:** Winterstein, J <J.Winterstein@lse.ac.uk>
**Subject:** Status of Media Relations request

To Whom It May Conern:

Jessica Winterstein, Deputy Head of Media Relations. forwarded my request for information to your office. Below is my request to Ms. Winterstein. Please advise on when I will receive a response. Thank you.

▮▮▮▮▮▮▮▮▮▮▮

***************************************************************************

I am working on an article about the controversy surrounding Republic of China in-exile President Tsai Ing-wen's LSE graduate thesis. Ms. Tsai filed her 1984 theis with the LSE Library in 2019 and that has generated much public interest in Taiwan. The name of the thesis is "Unfair Trade Practices and Safeguard Actions."

My questions, for publication, are:

1) What is the name and degree of Tsai Ing-wen's LSE Advisor?
2) What are the names of the thesis Examiners?
3) What is the date of the thesis oral review?
4) What is the date of the Examiner's signatures of approval?

If you are not the correct person to handle this information request please forward to the appropriate individual.

Thank you for your attention to this request.

# RE_-Tsai-Ing-Wen

**From:** Fisher,RW
**To:** Metcalfe,F; O'Connor,D; Smith,DAA
**Subject:** RE: Tsai Ing-Wen
**Date:** 09 October 2019 12:32:43
**Attachments:** image002.png
image003.png
image005.png

Thanks Fiona, I'll take that approach in future.

All the best,
Ross

**From:** Metcalfe,F
**Sent:** 09 October 2019 12:14
**To:** O'Connor,D <D.O'Connor@lse.ac.uk>; Fisher,RW <R.W.Fisher@lse.ac.uk>; Smith,DAA <D.A.A.Smith@lse.ac.uk>
**Subject:** Re: Tsai Ing-Wen

I agree with ignore and delete. Otherwise we keep feeding this.

**From:** O'Connor,D <D.O'Connor@lse.ac.uk>
**Sent:** Wednesday, October 9, 2019 9:54:22 AM
**To:** Fisher,RW <R.W.Fisher@lse.ac.uk>; Smith,DAA <D.A.A.Smith@lse.ac.uk>; Metcalfe,F <F.Metcalfe@lse.ac.uk>
**Subject:** Re: Tsai Ing-Wen

Thanks Ross.

I wonder if saying 'we consider this case closed' or 'final word' etc might be provocative to the trolls.

Probably worth deleting, I don't think many serious messages would go via the website.

**From:** Fisher,RW <R.W.Fisher@lse.ac.uk>
**Sent:** 09 October 2019 09:49
**To:** O'Connor,D <D.O'Connor@lse.ac.uk>; Smith,DAA <D.A.A.Smith@lse.ac.uk>; Metcalfe,F <F.Metcalfe@lse.ac.uk>
**Subject:** RE: Tsai Ing-Wen

Thanks Danny,

I agree that we shouldn't feed the trolls. Based on this feedback is there anything that you want to add to that statement? Even just to say this is our final word on this subject?

In future should we just delete these emails?

All the best,
Ross

**From:** O'Connor,D
**Sent:** 09 October 2019 09:41
**To:** Fisher,RW <R.W.Fisher@lse.ac.uk>; Smith,DAA <D.A.A.Smith@lse.ac.uk>; Metcalfe,F <F.Metcalfe@lse.ac.uk>
**Subject:** Re: Tsai Ing-Wen

I suppose this is the argument against putting up the statement online.

I don't think we should engage with any of this. The online statement is what we have to say about this. We haven't got anything else to say.

Danny

**From:** Fisher,RW <R.W.Fisher@lse.ac.uk>
**Sent:** 09 October 2019 09:35
**To:** O'Connor,D <D.O'Connor@lse.ac.uk>; Smith,DAA <D.A.A.Smith@lse.ac.uk>; Metcalfe,F <F.Metcalfe@lse.ac.uk>
**Subject:** Tsai Ing-Wen

Hi guys,

I guess someone put out another article about everyone's favourite alumna yesterday, because our inbox is suddenly full of complaints. What should the process be for these?

All the best
Ross

**Ross Fisher**
Digital Content Manager | Communications Division
The London School of Economics and Political Science
Houghton Street, London WC2A 2AE
+44 (0)20 7955 4658
: r.w.fisher@lse.ac.uk
lse.ac.uk

THE LONDON SCHOOL OF ECONOMICS AND POLITICAL SCIENCE

LSE is ranked #1 in Europe for social sciences
(QS World University Ranking 2019)

# Statement on the LSE website

| | |
|---|---|
| From: | O"Connor,D |
| To: | Shih,F |
| Subject: | Statement on the LSE website |
| Date: | 08 October 2019 13:09:00 |
| Attachments: | image002.png |
| | image003.png |
| | image005.png |

Dear Fang-long

To let you know, we are planning to put up a statement on our website later today where we can direct enquiries about Dr Tsai's PhD (as below)

It doesn't go into all the details being requested but provides an overview.

Best wishes,

Danny

### LSE statement on PhD of Dr Tsai Ing-wen

LSE has received a number of queries regarding the academic status of our alumna, Dr Tsai Ing-wen, President of Taiwan.

We can be clear the records of LSE and of the University of London - the degree awarding body at the time - confirm that Dr Tsai was correctly awarded a PhD in Law in 1984.

All degrees from that period were awarded via the University of London and the thesis would have been sent first to their Senate House Library. However, it has recently been discovered that the University of London Senate House Library are unable to find the hard copy of the thesis.

The Senate House Library records confirm that a copy was received and sent by them to the Institute for Advanced Legal Studies (IALS). There is a listing of Dr Tsai's thesis 'Unfair trade practices and safeguard actions' in the IALS index document "Legal Research in the United Kingdom 1905-1984", which was published in 1985.

Dr Tsai recently provided the LSE Library with a facsimile of a personal copy of the thesis, *Unfair trade practices and safeguard actions* which is available to view in the Library's Reading Room. We understand Dr Tsai has also provided a digital version of her personal copy to the National Central Library of Taiwan.

Daniel O'Connor
**Head of Media Relations | Communications Division**
The London School of Economics and Political Science
Houghton Street, London WC2A 2AE
t: +44 (0)20 7955 7417
e: oconnord@lse.ac.uk
lse.ac.uk

LSE is ranked #1 in Europe for social sciences
(QS World University Ranking 2019)

恶官 3

# Certificates of "Evils I" in Major Libraries Worldwide

# Library of Congress

**LIBRARY OF CONGRESS** | CATALOG

← Refine Your Search    1 of 1

BOOK
## E guan

Full Record    MARC Tags

**Personal name**
Zhang, Jing (Lawyer) author.
張靜 (Lawyer) author.

**Main title**
E guan / Zhang Jing, Li Zhenhua, Lin Bingsong he zhu ; Peng Wenzheng zhu bian
总官 / 張靜, 李震華, 林秉松合著 ; 彭文正主編

**Edition**
Chu ban
初版

**Published/Produced**
United States : Thesis7ting LLC, 2022

Request this Item    LC Find It

| | |
|---|---|
| LCCN Permalink | https://lccn.loc.gov/2022400496 |
| Description | 480 pages : illustrations, facsimiles ; 24 cm |
| ISBN | 9798986219301 |
| LC classification | DS799.849.C353 Z42 2022+ |
| Related names | Peng, Dennis, editor. |
| Summary | This book chronicles the event behind Taiwan President Tsai Ing-wen's academic fraud and how she obtained a fake PH. D. from the London School of Economics and Political Science. Author Dr. Dennis Peng, in his quest for truth, has been politically persecuted for his thorough investigation into the matter. |
| LC Subjects | Tsai, Ing-wen. |
| Other Subjects | 蔡英文 |
| Browse by shelf order | DS799.849.C353 |
| LCCN | 2022400496 |

# British Library

**Gmail**

THESIS7TING LLC <thesis7ting.llc@gmail.com>

## Donation 2804: RE: Book donation to British Library

2022年12月22日 晚上7:17

Just to let you know that we have received your book. I will send it to be added to our collection.

This process can often take a few months. The only way to check when it becomes available is to search our public catalogue 'Explore' on a regular basis. http://explore.bl.uk

Thank you for donating to the British Library.

Kind regards

Brian

Brian Elvidge

Donation Coordinators

Content Development Implementation

Building 2, Room 2.07

The British Library,

Boston Spa,

Wetherby,

West Yorkshire.

LS23 7BQ

donations@bl.uk

# National Library of Australia

**M Gmail**  THESIS7TING LLC <thesis7ting.llc@gmail.com>

**NLAacq85761 National Library of Australia - collection offer update**
2 封邮件

2022年12月2日 上午11:58

Update on offer #: NLAacq85761

## National Library of Australia

Update on offer #: NLAacq85761

**Our update is:**

Dear Sandy Lin

Thank you for offering "Evils" to the National Library of Australia. The Library would be delighted to accept this material. From your description, I can see that the material would be a valuable addition to the Library's collections and a useful resource for researchers. Your generosity in donating this material is greatly appreciated.

In terms of transferring the material to the Library, we prefer that donors send items in a padded bag or small box, via Australia Post, to the address below. Please reference this letter and quote NLAacq85761.

Could you please fill in our NLA donation slip (please see attached) and send it with the materials to:

Collection Donations, Collect & Acquire
National Library of Australia
Parkes Place
Canberra ACT 2600

Please feel free to contact me if you have any questions or concerns.

Yours sincerely

Jie Chen
Senior Library Officer
Curatorial & Collection Research
National Library of Australia
Number of documents attached to this message:1
*Attached documents may be listed at the beginning or end of this email*

198  The biggest degree fraud case in human history

# Harvard Library

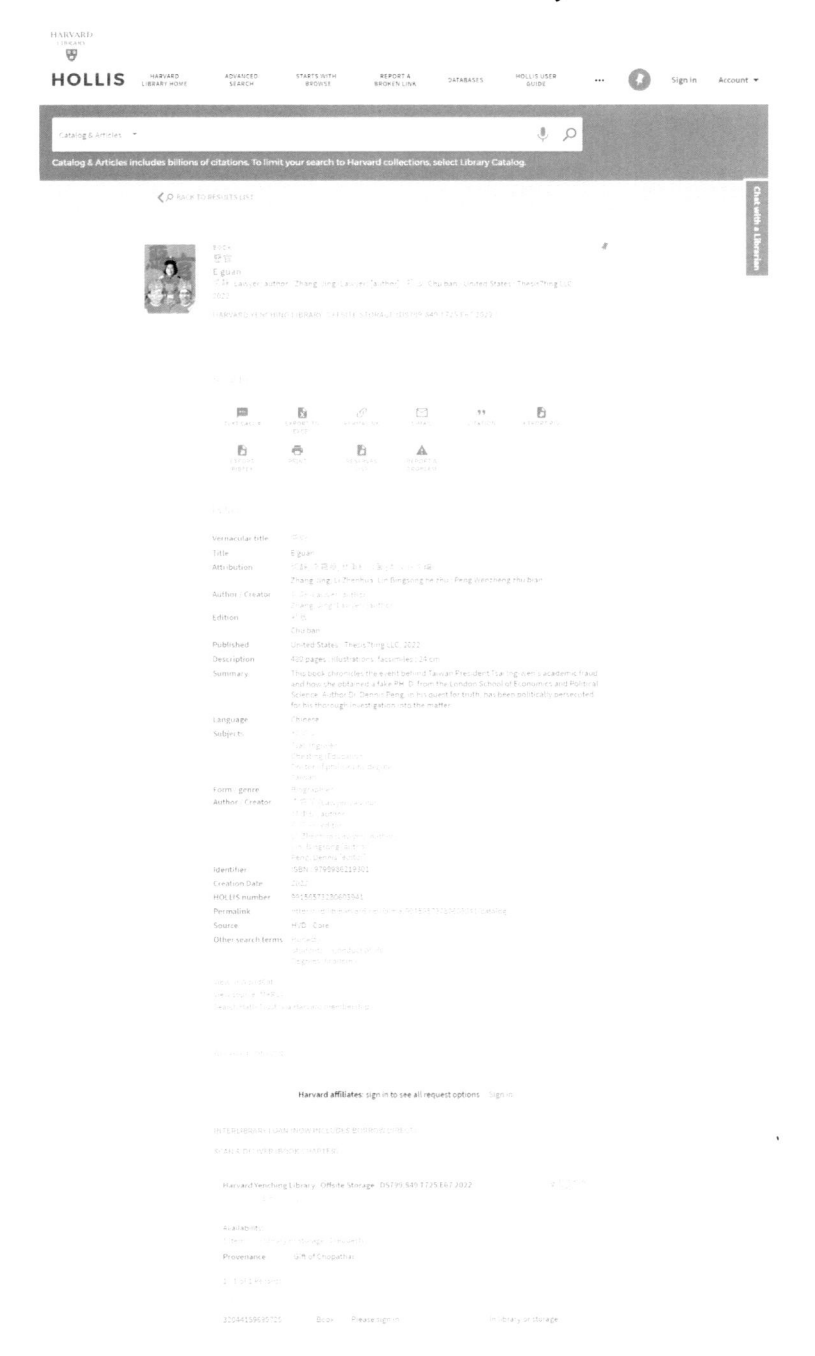

The biggest degree fraud case in human history    199

# Princeton University Library

PRINCETON UNIVERSITY LIBRARY
PRINCETON, NEW JERSEY 08544
TEL: (609) 258-3182 FAX: (609) 258-4573

Nov. 14, 2022

On behalf of the Trustees of Princeton University, I am pleased to acknowledge the receipt of

張靜，李震華，林秉松合著，　　　惡官　　　(Thesis7ting. 2022)

which you have presented to the University Library. In compliance with Internal Revenue Service Code, we must state that we provided neither goods nor services in return for this kind gift.

Please accept our most cordial thanks.

Sincerely,

Joshua Seufert
Chinese Studies Librarian
The East Asian Library and
　　The Gest Collection

辱蒙厚贈 嘉惠學林 隆情銘感 謹函布謝

# Stanford Libraries

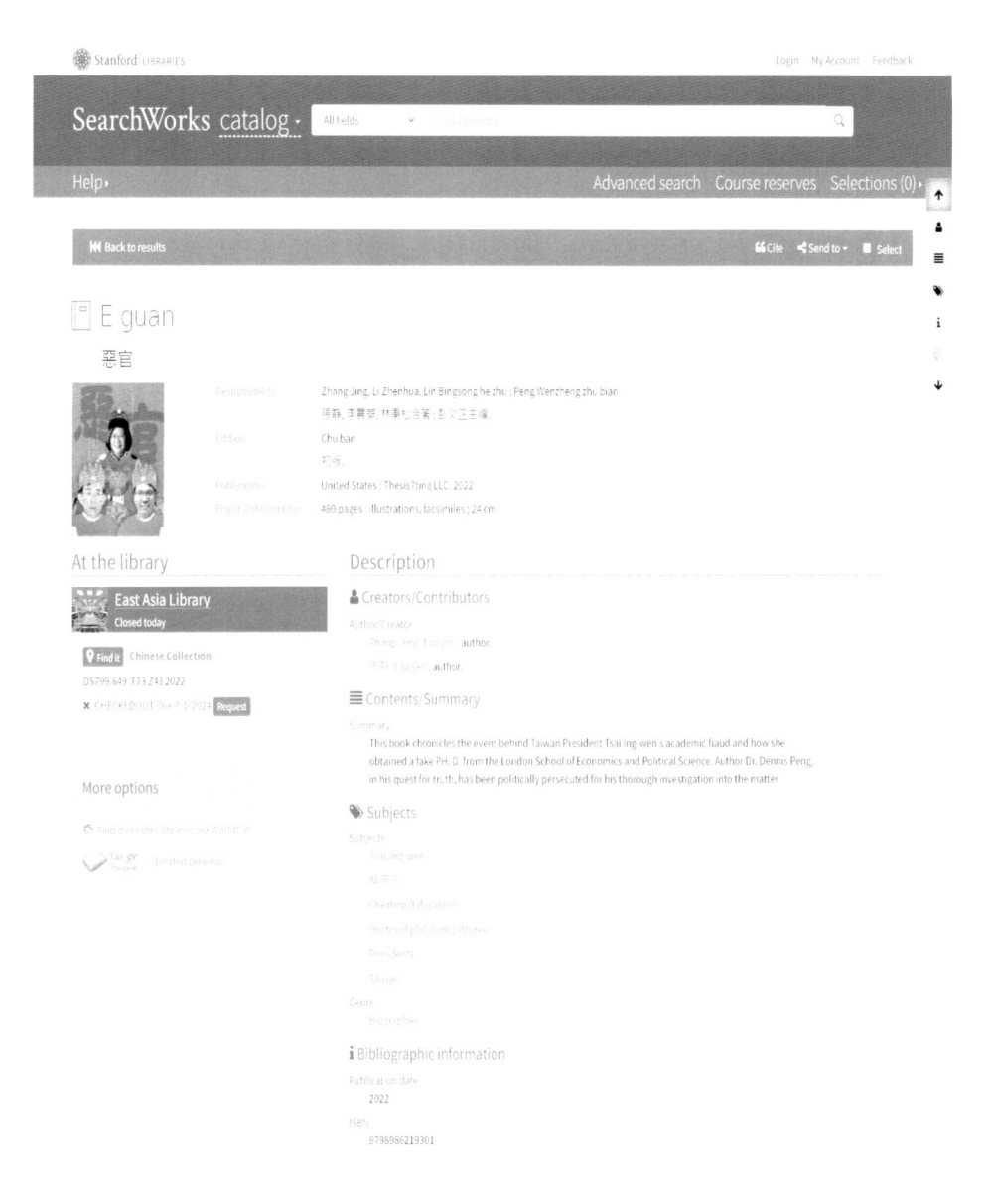

## E guan
### 惡官

**Publication:** United States : Thesis7ting LLC, 2022

**Physical description:** 480 pages : illustrations, facsimiles ; 24 cm

### Description

**Summary:**
This book chronicles the event behind Taiwan President Tsai Ing-wen's academic fraud and how she obtained a fake Ph.D. from the London School of Economics and Political Science. Author Dr. Dennis Peng, in his quest for truth, has been politically persecuted for his thorough investigation into the matter.

**Publication date:** 2022

**ISBN:** 9796986219301

The biggest degree fraud case in human history

# Yale University Library

Yale UNIVERSITY LIBRARY

We gratefully acknowledge receipt of the gift mentioned below and extend to you our sincere appreciation.

For the Chinese Collection
居官

Sincerely,

Michael Meng
Head, East Asia Library and Librarian for Chinese Studies
212 Sterling Memorial Library
Yale University Library
Phone: 203-432-4438
michael.meng@yale.edu

# Penn Libraries - University of Pennsylvania

*UNIVERSITY of PENNSYLVANIA*

I write to thank you for your gift of 《惡官》 to the University of Pennsylvania Library. We very much appreciate your interest in our collection and your generosity in supporting us.

Sincerely,

Brian Vivier
Chinese Studies Librarian

# Columbia University Libraries

**? COLUMBIA UNIVERSITY**
Weatherhead East Asian Institute

November 16, 2022

I received Mr. Peng's book, 《惡官》. Thank you so much for sending it. I'm writing you by mail because I have lost your email address. The book arrived last week. It is very kind of you to send it.

Best,

*Andy*

Andrew J. Nathan
Class of 1919 Professor of Political Science

# UCLA Library

**UCLA** Library

Richard C. Rudolph East Asian Library

January 5, 2023

Thank you very much for donating the following publication to the UCLA East Asian Library.

惡官 / 張靜, 李震華, 林秉松合著; 彭文正主編

We have included this book in our collection, and made it available to our faculty, students, researchers and general library users. Please accept my sincere appreciation.

Truly yours,

*Hong Cheng*

Hong Cheng, Ph.D.
Chinese Studies Librarian

# UC San Diego Library

## UC San Diego

December 15, 2022

Thank you for your donation of the following title to the UC San Diego Library's collection.

惡官

As you may know, we have for many years been building and shaping a Chinese-language collection in the humanities and social sciences covering China, Hong Kong, and Taiwan. This collection is a regional and national resource for Chinese Studies researchers and students throughout San Diego County, the state of California, and the U.S.

Your donation will most likely be used by students in UC San Diego's classes on politics and legal studies and faculty and graduate students who research the same topics.

Thank you again for your donation to the Library at UC San Diego.

Xi Chen
Sally T. WongAvery Librarian of Chinese Studies and East Asia Collection Strategist

# University of Michigan Library

THE UNIVERSITY OF MICHIGAN
THE ASIA LIBRARY

920 N. UNIVERSITY
ANN ARBOR, MICHIGAN 48109-1205 U.S.A.
734 764-0406    FAX 734 647-2885
http://asia.lib.umich.edu

October 10, 2022

    On behalf of the Regents of the University of Michigan, we have the honor to acknowledge with gratitude receipt of 惡官 at the Asia Library. This book will be accessible from the University Library catalogue. We believe your generous gift will benefit not only academic community at our university, but also scholars outside the University of Michigan.

With thanks and kind regards,

Liangyu Fu, Ph.D.

# University of Wisconsin-Madison Libraries

November 16, 2022

Thank you for your gift to the libraries at the University of Wisconsin-Madison. We appreciate your generosity and thoughtfulness in donating this material to the General Library System. It is with your help that we continue to build useful and distinctive collections for the University community.

We gratefully acknowledge your contribution:

Peng, Dennis, author.
惡官 /張靜, 李震華, 林秉松合著 ; 彭文正主編.
E guan / Zhang Jing, Li Zhenhua, Lin Bingsong he zhu ; Peng Wenzheng zhu bian.
初版.
Chu ban.

With appreciation,

*Lisa R Carter*

Lisa R. Carter
Vice Provost for Libraries

cc: Nancy Graff Schultz
Elizabeth Lightfoot
Anlin Yang

*This gift is made unconditionally and is free from any restrictions, obligations, or arrangements.*

*The IRS further requires us to state that you have received no goods or services in exchange for this contribution, or the value of any items received in exchange for this contribution falls within the definition of "low cost articles" under section 513(h)(2) of the Internal Revenue Service Code.*

General Library System

# Cornell University Library

Wason Collection on East Asia
Cornell University
171 Kroch Library
Ithaca, NY 14853

Telephone: 607 255-4357
Fax: 607 255-8438
E-mail: wason.collection@cornell.edu

January 5, 2023

This letter is to acknowledge that the Wason Collection on East Asia at Cornell University Library has received the following title

《惡官》第一卷，彭文正 主編，張靜 李震華 林秉松 合著，Thesis7ting LLC, USA 出版

We greatly appreciate your generosity and believe that our patrons will certainly benefit from your donations. We look forward to your continuing support for our library and wish you the best.

Sincerely yours,

Jing Carlson

# University of Washington Libraries

**UNIVERSITY LIBRARIES**
UNIVERSITY of WASHINGTON
Gifts Program

6 November 2022

On behalf of the University of Washington Libraries, it is my privilege to express our appreciation for your gift to the Tateuchi East Asia Library. We gratefully acknowledge the 10 June 2022 receipt of 惡官.

The UW Libraries is the heart of our great university. Our facilities, services, and collections nurture the dynamic teaching, learning, and research that are the hallmark of the University of Washington. Students and scholars from around the world rely on our 9.5 million volumes and vast electronic resources for information and inspiration. Our mission to advance intellectual discovery and enrich the quality of life by connecting people with knowledge is not just an idea, it is what we do. But we cannot do it without the support of people like you. Together we are fostering research and engagement that transform lives and create a better world.

Thank you again for your generosity.

Sincerely yours,

Carolyn H. Aamot
Head, Gifts Program / Content Manager

*The University of Washington provided no goods or services in exchange for this gift.*

# Bodleian Libraries, University of Oxford

Gmail - Book donation to The Bodleian Libraries.

**M Gmail**

THESIS7TING LLC <thesis7ting.llc@gmail.com>

## Book donation to The Bodleian Libraries.

UAS Development Bodleian <development@bodleian.ox.ac.uk>  2022年12月21日 下午6:14
收件者: THESIS7TING LLC <thesis7ting.llc@gmail.com>, UAS Development Bodleian <development@bodleian.ox.ac.uk>

Dear Sandy

Thank you very much for your intention of donating the book you mention below, we will be delighted to receive it!

**At the moment the only way to donate books is by post.**

Please send it to this address with a brief accompanying message explaining it is a gift from you:

Acquisitions Services
Collections & Resource Description (C & RD)
Bodleian Libraries
Osney One Building
Osney Mead
Oxford
OX2 0EW
UK

The Acquisitions Team will acknowledge receipt and thank you personally.

Many thanks once again.
Best wishes,
Emanuele

**Emanuele Faccenda**
**Development Coordinator – Gardens, Libraries and Museums**

Bodleian Libraries, Clarendon Building

Broad street, Oxford, OX1 3BG United Kingdom
E emanuele.faccenda@devoff.ox.ac.uk

https://www.development.ox.ac.uk/bodleian-libraries
Twitter: twitter.com/OxfordGiving

Facebook: www.facebook.com/OxfordGiving

To find out more about how we collect, store and process your data, including your rights and choices, please read our privacy notice. If you no longer wish to hear from us, please let us know at database@devoff.ox.ac.uk

[隱藏引用文字]

# SOAS Library, University of London

**Gmail**

THESIS7TING LLC <thesis7ting.llc@gmail.com>

**Book donation to SOAS Library.**

2022年12月13日 晚上9:35

com>

Dear Sandy,

Thank you for your kind offer.

We would be happy to take on this book.

Please could you post to:

Ludi Price
SOAS Library
Thornhaugh St,
Russell Square,
London WC1H 0XG

Before sending, please read our donation policy and make sure you are happy with it. We would also be grateful if you could fill out our donation form, and send it with your donation.

Please do let me know if you have any further questions.

Best wishes,
Ludi

212 The biggest degree fraud case in human history

悪官 3

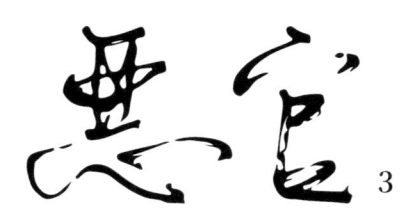

**Appendix**

214 The biggest degree fraud case in human history

- In 2011, Tsai Ing-wen, then the chairperson of the Democratic Progressive Party, planned to run for the 2012 Taiwan presidential election. On June 7, she led a delegation to LSE, meeting with then British Lord, former LSE director Anthony Giddens, and David Held, who was the supervising professor for Muammar Gaddafi's son in a "degree scandal". Subsequently, in July 2011, LSE initiated its first arrangement regarding the non-existence of Tsai's thesis.

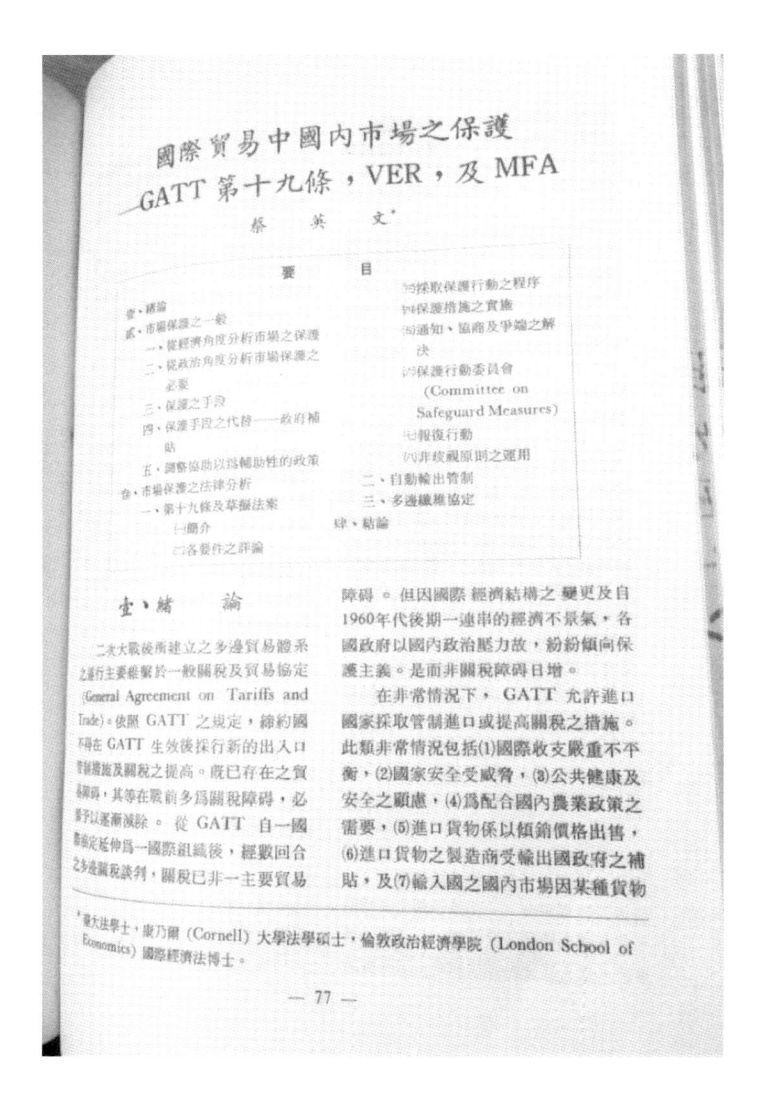

- In June 1983, Tsai Ing-wen published an article in the Law Journal of National Chengchi University in Taiwan. At that time, she hadn't even submitted her claimed doctoral thesis to the LSE yet, but she identified herself as a Doctor of International Economic Law from LSE in the journal. This entire article was translated verbatim into a chapter of her so-called doctoral thesis.

- On October 20, 1983, Tsai Ing-wen submitted an article titled "On the Anti-Dumping Tax for Our Color TVs Exported to the US" to the United Daily News in Taiwan, identifying herself as a Doctor of International Economic Law from the LSE. However, this was just four days after LSE claimed she had attended her doctoral Viva examination on October 16, 1983.

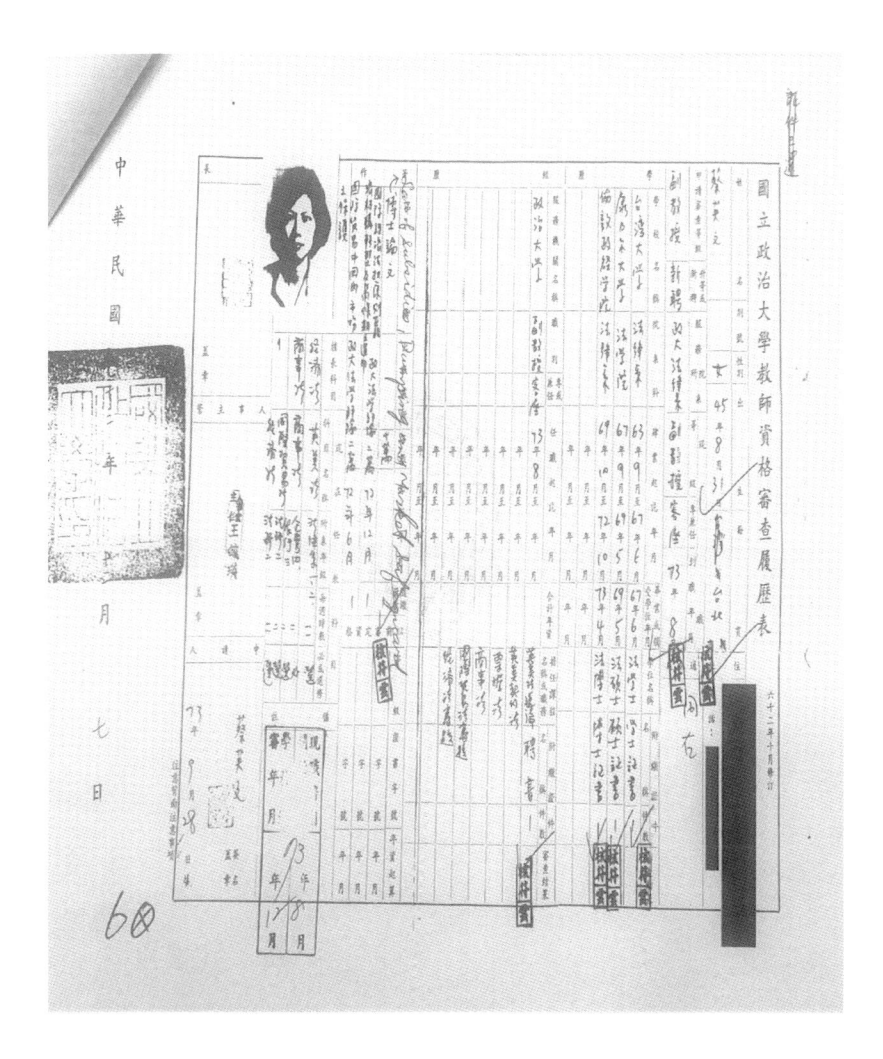

- Due to Tsai Ing-wen's sealing of her curriculum vitae and promotion materials from National Chengchi University, Professor Emeritus He Defen of the College of Law at National Taiwan University filed an administrative lawsuit against the Ministry of Education. As a result, she obtained Tsai's teacher qualification review CV from September 1984. At that time, the doctoral thesis title filled out by Tsai herself was "Law of Subsidies, Dumping, and Market Safeguards," not "*Unfair Trade Practices and Safeguard Actions.*"

218   The biggest degree fraud case in human history

- In her book " 洋蔥炒蛋與小英便當 ," published on October 25, 2011, Tsai Ing-wen wrote that the title of her doctoral thesis was: *"Unfair Trade Practices and Safeguard for Domestic Market."*

- In Tsai Ing-wen's autobiography " 洋蔥炒蛋與小英便當 ," there is a photo of her with her elder sister, Tsai Ying-ling. The caption reads: "For my doctoral thesis defense, my sister specially flew to the UK to accompany me." However, in 2019, netizens identified the background of the photo, including the streetlights and vehicles, and accurately determined that the location was St. Paul's Cathedral in Boston, USA. Tsai Ing-wen promptly changed the caption in the e-book version of her autobiography to: "A photo with my elder sister, Tsai Ying-ling."

- In June 2019, Tsai Ing-wen placed her so-called "thesis" in the Women's Library of the LSE for public viewing. However, there were strict restrictions on accessing it. When interviewed by the media, Tsai expressed surprise, saying, "Is that so?" indicating she was unaware of the situation. Yet, the tummy band on Tsai's "thesis" at LSE clearly stated that the restrictions were imposed by the author herself.

(a) 1984　　　　　　　　　(b) 2010　　　　　　　　　(c) 2015

- Despite the clear regulations of the University of London that a doctoral degree certificate can only be reissued once in a lifetime and that an application requires a notarized statement of loss, Tsai Ing-wen has had her degree certificate reissued twice, resulting in three certificates in total.

(圖二：LSE學生紀錄)

- On September 4, 2019, the Taiwan Presidential Office Spokesperson's Office posted Tsai Ing-wen's student record on Facebook. The remarks clearly indicated that Tsai "withdrew from the course" on November 10, 1982. Additionally, there were no records of fees paid or a Supervisor for her in 1983.

The biggest degree fraud case in human history 223

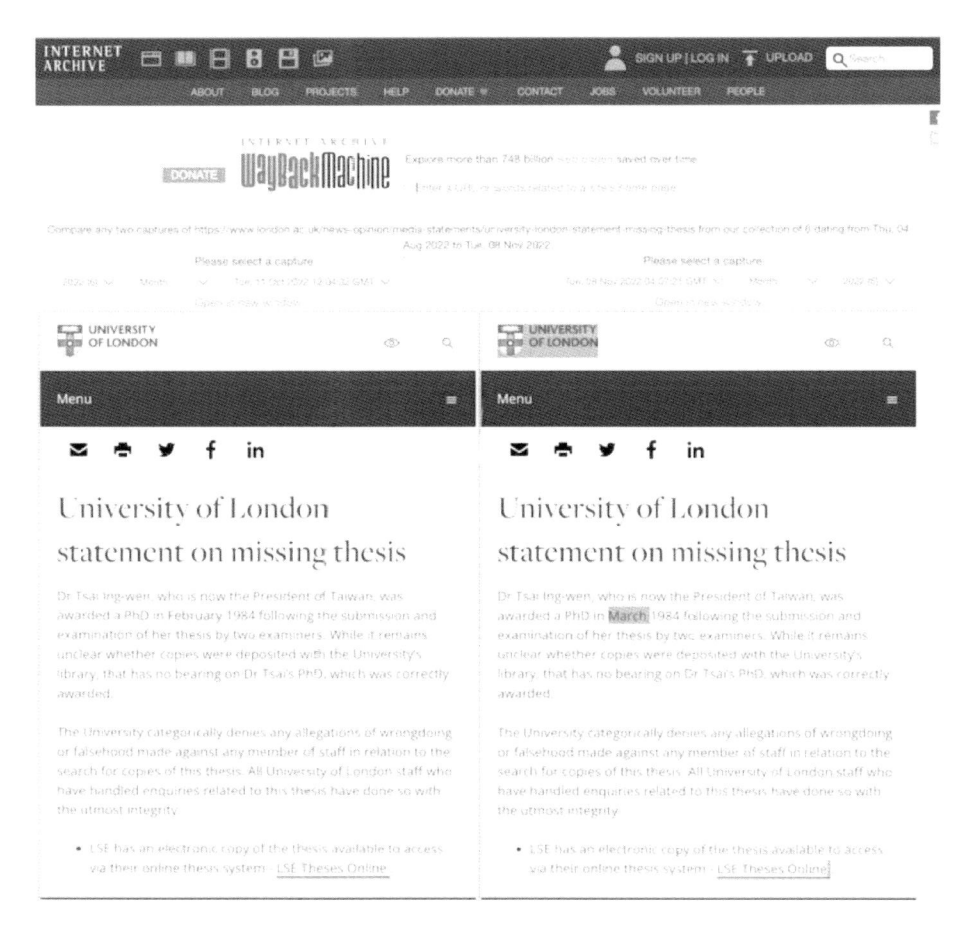

- In February 2022, the University of London issued a statement regarding Tsai Ing-wen's missing thesis. Initially, they claimed that Tsai obtained her degree in February 1984. However, it was later discovered that the webpage was discreetly altered to state March 1984.

In considering this balancing test, I have taken into account the following factors:

- the potential harm or distress that disclosure may cause
- whether the information is already in the public domain
- whether the information is already known to some individuals
- whether the individual expressed concern to the disclosure, and
- the reasonable expectations of the individual.

In my view, a key issue is whether the individual concerned has a reasonable expectation that their information will not be disclosed. These expectations can be shaped by factors such as an individual's general expectation of privacy, whether the information relates to an employee in their professional role or to them as individuals, and the purpose for which they provided their personal data.

The requested information is associated with an individual in a private/personal capacity. I am satisfied that the individual concerned (the student) would have the reasonable expectation that their personal data – that is; specific information about their thesis – who examined it and when - would not be disclosed to world at large in response to a FOI request.

I consider it likely that disclosing this information would cause that individual a degree of damage or distress.

You have not presented an argument for the information's disclosure that is sufficiently compelling to override the data subject's rights and freedoms.

You have also noted that UL did not discuss the matter of the examiners' personal data. However, as the regulator whose role is to safeguard personal data, the Commissioner will actively consider whether releasing information would disclose anyone's personal data – whether a public authority has considered it or not. In this case, releasing the information you have requested would disclose the examiners' personal data (their names). Again, I am satisfied that they would not expect this to be disclosed in response to a FOIA request and that disclosure would not be lawful.

Having therefore considered all the circumstances, I consider that your legitimate interest in the information in question is insufficient to outweigh the data subjects' fundamental rights and freedoms. I therefore consider that there is no Article 6 basis for processing and so the disclosure of the information would not be lawful.

Given the above conclusion that disclosure would be unlawful, it is not necessary to separately consider whether disclosure would be fair or transparent.

- On March 23, 2020, the UK Information Commissioner's Office (ICO) responded to Michael Richardson's Freedom of Information Act (FOIA) request regarding the members of Tsai Ing-wen's viva panel. The ICO replied that "disclosing the information about the viva panel would inflict harm or distress upon Tsai."

- Records Management, 11 January 2022

Dear Li Xing Chen

Many thanks for your patience in waiting for an answer to your request during our University closure period.

I am sorry but the University of London does not hold any information relating to information held by LSE about Ing-Wen Tsai. I am unable to give you any information in response to your questions about this.

The primary record for PhD awards is held by the Member Institution, not the University of London.

Kind regards

Suzie Mereweather
Head of Data Protection and Information Compliance

University of London   Senate House
Malet Street   London   WC1E 7HU   UK
[email address]
+44 (0)20 7862 5844   www.london.ac.uk

show quoted sections

- On January 11, 2022, Suzie Mereweather, the Information Protection Manager at the University of London, publicly responded to inquiries about the availability of information related to Tsai Ing-wen's doctoral viva at the University of London on the WDTK platform. The University of London denied having such information, stating that it is preserved by member institutions.

226   The biggest degree fraud case in human history

惡官 3

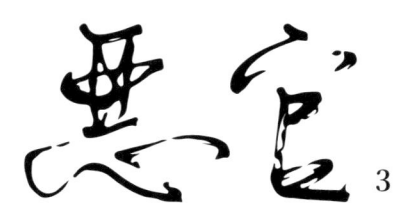

# List of Individuals Involved in LSE Thesis-gate Scandal

## Daniel Gulliford

Admin Assistant | Directorate (Former)
ASCRU Administrator and NIHR SSCR Capacity-Building Officer | CPEC ( Present )
The London School of Economics and Political Science
Houghton Street, London WC2A 2AE
t: +44 (0)20 7852 3601
e: D.J.Gulliford@lse.ac.uk

## Baroness Minouche Shafik

President of the London School
of Economics and Political Science
( Sep. 2017~June. 2023)
President of Columbia University ( Jul. 2023~Present)

## Nicola Wright

Director of LSE Library ( Jan. 2015 - Dec. 2022 )
LSE Library
10 Portugal Street London WC2A 2HD
e: n.c.wright@lse.ac.uk

## Fang-long Shih

Co-Director, Taiwan Research Programme
The London School of Economics and Political Science
Houghton Street, London WC2A 2AE


## Shuma Begum

Research Degrees Officer | PhD Academy
The London School of Economics and Political Science
Houghton Street London WC2A 2AE


## Sue Donnelly

LSE Archivist | Secretary`s Division
The London School of Economics and Political Science
Houghton Street, London WC2A 2AE
t: +44 (0)20 7955 2840
e: s.donnelly@lse.ac.uk


## Liz Jaggs

Head of Executive Support (Feb. 2019 - Nov. 2022)
Head of Communications ( Jun. 2022 - Present)
LSE Philanthropy and Global Engagement
Houghton Street, London WC2A 2AE
t: +44 (0)20 7955 7783
e: l.jaggs@lse.ac.uk

## Simeon Underwood

Academic Registrar and Director of Academic
(Retired in 2015 )
The London School of Economics and Political Science
Houghton Street, London WC2A 2AE

## Ross Fisher

Digital Content Manager ｜ Communications Division
The London School of Economics and Political Science
( Aug. 2018~Oct. 2010 )
Content Editor, Historic England Appointment  ( Present )

## Simon Hix

Academic Director of LSE ( 2017 - 2018 )
Pro-Director for Research of LSE ( 2019 - 2021)
EUI Stein Rokkan Chair in Comparative Politics
 (2021 - Present)
e: S.Hix@lse.ac.uk

## Louisa Green

Research Degrees Manager of LSE (Former)
Executive Director for Student Services of Kingston University (Present)

## O'Connor

Head of Media Relations | Communications Division
The London School of Economics and Political Science
Houghton Street, London WC2A 2AE
t: +44 (0)20 7955 7417
e: d.o'connor@lse.ac.uk

## Mark Thomson

Academic Registrar | Academic Registrar's Division
The London School of Economics and Political Science
Houghton Street, London WC2A 2AE
e: m.t.thomson@lse.ac.uk

## Wilson

Enquiry Services Manager | Academic Services
LSE Library
10 Portugal Street London WC2A 2HD
t: +44 (0)2079227475
e: clive.wilson@lse.ac.uk

## Charlotte Kelloway

Media Relations Manager | Communications Division
The London School of Economics and Political Science
Houghton Street, London WC2A 2AE
t: +44 (0)20 7955 6558
e: c.kelloway@lse.ac.uk

## Fiona Metcalfe

Director of Communications | Communications Division
The London School of Economics and Political Science
Houghton Street, London WC2A 2AE
t: +44 (0)20 3486 2892
e: f.metcalfe@lse.ac.uk

## Nancy Graham

Associate Director | Collections and Academic Services
LSE Library
10 Portugal Street, London WC2A 2HD
e: n.graham1@lse.ac.uk

## Alex Huang

Spokesperson of the President
Office of the President, ROC ( Taiwan )
No.122, Sec.1,Chongqing S. Rd, Taipei City, Taiwan

## Remi Adeyemi

Executive Assistant to the Academic Registrar | Academic Registrar's Division
The London School of Economics and Political Science
Houghton Street, London WC2A 2AE
t: +44 (0)20 7955 7121
e: r.adeyemi@lse.ac.uk

## Marcus Cerny

Deputy Director | PhD Academy ( Nov. 2016~Nov. 2021 )
The London School of Economics and Political Science
Houghton Street London WC2A 2AE
e: m.w.cerny@lse.ac.uk


## Beth Clark

Associate Director | Digital Scholarship and Innovation
LSE Library
10 Portugal Street London WC2A 2HD
e: b.clark1@lse.ac.uk


## Ruth Orson

Library Assistant, Research Support Services |
 LSE Research Online
LSE Library
10 Portugal Street, London WC2A 2HD
t: +44 (0)020 7955 3528
e: R.Orson@lse.ac.uk

## Kevin Haynes

Head of Legal Team | Legal Team, Secretary's Division
The London School of Economics and Political Science
Houghton Street, London WC2A 2AE
t: +44 (0)20 79557823
e: K.J.Haynes@lse.ac.uk

## Refel Ismail

Senior Legal Counsel | Legal Team, Secretary`s Division
The London School of Economics and Political Science
Houghton Street, London WC2A 2AE
t: +44 (0)20 7955 6171
e: r.ismail@lse.ac.uk

## Chris Kendrick

Deputy Director of Alumni & Supporter Engagement |
LSE Philanthropy and Global Engagement
The London School of Economics and Political Science
Houghton Street, London WC2A 2AE
t:+44 (0)20 7107 5200
e: c.kendrick@lse.ac.uk

## Jessica Winterstein

Deputy Head of Media Relations | Media Relations team
The London School of Economics and Political Science
Houghton Street, London WC2A 2AE
t: +44 (0)20 7107 5025
e: j.winterstein@lse.ac.uk

## Sue Windebank

Senior Media Relations Manager | Media Relations team
The London School of Economics and Political Science
Houghton Street, London WC2A 2AE
t: +44 (0)20 7849 4624
e: s.windebank@lse.ac.uk

## Joanna Bale

Senior Media Relations Manager | Media Relations team
The London School of Economics and Political Science
Houghton Street, London WC2A 2AE
t: +44 (0)20 7955 7440
e: j.m.bale@lse.ac.uk

## Marta Gajewska

Executive Assistant to Baroness Minouche Shafik, LSE Director ( Feb. 2019 - Oct. 2021)
Executive Manager CEO Office of The Association of Commonwealth Universities (Present)

## Simeon Underwood

Academic Registrar and Director of Academic
(Retired in 2015 )
The London School of Economics and Political Science
Houghton Street, London WC2A 2AE

## Rachael Maguire

Information and Records Manager | Secretary's Division
The London School of Economics and Political Science
t: +44(0)20 7849 4622
e: R.E.Maguire@lse.ac.uk

## Mike Pearson
Head of Digital | Communications Division
(Sep. 2018 - Mar. 2022)
The London School of Economics and Political Science
Houghton Street, London WC2A 2AE
e: m.k.pearson@lse.ac.uk


## Inderbir Bhullar
Curator for Economics and Social Policy
LSE Library
10 Portugal Street London WC2A 2HD
e: i.bhullar@lse.ac.uk

## Louise Nadal

School Secretary | Secretary's Division
The London School of Economics and Political Science
Houghton Street, London WC2A 2AE
t: +44(0)20 7849 4959
e: L.Nadal@lse.ac.uk

## Maria Bell

Learning Support Services Manager
LSE Library
10 Portugal Street London WC2A 2HD
e: m.bell@lse.ac.uk

## Heather Dawson
Librarian
LSE Library
10 Portugal Street London WC2A 2HD
e: h.dawson@lse.ac.uk

## Andra Fry
Information Specialist
LSE Library
10 Portugal Street London WC2A 2HD
e: a.e.fry@lse.ac.uk

## Sonia Gomes

Librarian
LSE Library
10 Portugal Street London WC2A 2HD
e: s.gomes@lse.ac.uk

## Anna Towlson

Archives and Special Collections Manager
LSE Library
10 Portugal Street London WC2A 2HD

## Dr Paul Horsler

Librarian LSE Library
10 Portugal Street London WC2A 2HD
e: p.n.horsler@lse.ac.uk

## Ridhwaan Hussain

Financial Planning Analyst | Financial Division
The London School of Economics and Political Science
Houghton Street, London WC2A 2AE
e: R.Hussain2@lse.ac.uk


## Dr Gillian Murphy

Curator for Equality, Rights and Citizenship
LSE Library
10 Portugal Street London WC2A 2HD
e: g.e.murphy@lse.ac.uk


## Ellen Wilkinson

Librarian
LSE Library
10 Portugal Street London WC2A 2HD
e: e.wilkinson@lse.ac.uk

## Professor Rita Astuti

Professor of Social Anthropology |
Department of Anthropology
The London School of Economics and Political Science
Houghton Street, London WC2A 2AE
e: r.astuti@lse.ac.uk


## Professor Max Schulze

Professor of Economic History |
Department of Economic History
The London School of Economics and Political Science
Houghton Street, London WC2A 2AE
t: +44 (0)2 7955 6784
e: m.s.schulze@lse.ac.uk


## Nicola Foster

Department Manager (interim) |
School of Public Policy
The London School of Economics and Political Science
Houghton Street, London WC2A 2AE
e: N.K.Foster@lse.ac.uk


## Matthew Brack

PhD Academy | Assistant Director
The London School of Economics and Political Science
Houghton Street, London WC2A 2AE
e: m.brack@lse.ac.uk

# Epilogue

As the *Evils III* is published (November 2023), Tsai continues to serve her final six months as the President of Taiwan. Meanwhile, Nemat "Minouche" Shafik, the former Director of the London School of Economics and Political Science, has taken up the role of President at Columbia University in the United States. Others involved in this Taiwan-UK academic fraud scandal, who played roles of feigned ignorance, fabricated evidence, deceit, and destruction of proof, are still in Taipei and London. They can be seen donning Burberry trench coats, living tranquil, insipid, and nefarious lives…

彭文正

11-10-23